Snatches of O'Daniel, Hamilton, and Allied Ancestry and History in Maryland and Kentucky

Snatches of O'Daniel, Hamilton, and Allied Ancestry and History in Maryland and Kentucky

VICTOR FRANCIS O'DANIEL

COMMONWEALTH BOOK COMPANY
ST. MARTIN, OHIO

Originally published by the Rosary Press in 1933. This edition copyright © 2024 by Commonwealth Book Company.

All rights reserved. No part of this book may be reproduced in any form or by any means without the prior written consent of the publisher, excepting brief quotes used in reviews.
Printed in the United States of America.

ISBN: 978-1-948986-75-5

CONTENTS

FOREWORD	5
THE O'DANIELS AND THE O'BRIENS	11
THE CAMBRONS AND THE MONTGOMERYS	35
THE HAMILTONS AND THE McATEES	49
THE SPALDINGS, THE ABELLS, AND THE O'BRYANS	72
THE EDELENS	86
SUMMARY OF DIRECT GENERATIONS	96
CONCLUSION	100

ILLUSTRATIONS

FORMER HOME OF MR. AND MRS. R. J. O'DANIEL	22
MR. AND MRS. R. J. O'DANIEL................	28
SISTER FRANCESCA O'DANIEL	28
THE REST OF THE O'DANIEL FAMILY..........	29

FOREWORD

This little book has been written at the frequent and urgent request of nephews, nieces, and friends. Had its author only taken the pains, in years long past, to seek more information from his mother and maternal grandmother, and to note down what was learned from them, the work could have been made more complete, as well as more exact in places. They were both exceptionally well informed on their family lines. Some of the grandmother's brothers and sisters were born in the State of Maryland, though she herself first saw the light of day in Kentucky. As it is, we owe to these two immediate progenitors not a little of what is stated in our pages.

Another source of information was Thomas W. Simms, who died in Springfield, Kentucky, some years ago. Born about 1830, a grandson of *Benedict Joseph* and *Alethea (Abell) Spalding,* who went out to that state from Maryland in 1790, and reared in the very midst of the writer's relations there, Mr. Simms had every opportunity of learning about them. Besides, he was unusually well versed in such things. He lived to be a nonagenarian, retaining a fine mind and memory until the end. A still more helpful source, although he belonged to practically the next generation, was the late Benedict E. Cambron. In Mr. Cambron's veins ran the blood of every line mentioned in these pages, except that of the O'Daniels; and he had many relations of that name. He was born and reared in the "Cambron neighborhood" mentioned in the first paper, and on the edge of the "Hamilton neighborhood" referred to in the same place. In fact, his mother was Harriet Hamilton. We remember her well. She was a first cousin of our own mother. Throughout his life Benedict Cambron was keenly interested in genealogy, and he kept in close touch with his kinsfolk. Thus he possessed a really marvellous knowledge of the various family connections in his part of Kentucky. His memory for facts, names, and dates was extraordinary. All this rendered him an authority to whom not a few genealogists had recourse in their researches. A comparison of his statements, which were noted down, with the extant church registers at Saint Rose's, near Springfield, the Washington County records at Springfield itself, and other documents, whenever possible, practically always showed them to be correct. If he were in doubt, he did not hesitate to say that he was not certain.

The *Archives of Maryland* and *The Maryland Calendar of Wills* were of great help in tracing the families before the historic Catholic exodus from the former Lord Baltimore Colony, or Maryland, for Kentucky, which began in 1785. Unfortunately, neither of these works has been brought down far enough for some of the data needed for this little volume. A few other books on the history of the Maryland Colony and the early state contributed a mite of aid. Furthermore, some years ago, while searching for other information in the records at Leonardtown (Saint Mary's County), La Plata (Charles County), Upper Marlboro (Prince George's County), Rockville (Montgomery County), and elsewhere, as well as in the state records at Annapolis, the writer kept an eye out for whatever might throw any light on his family lines. But the pressure of the work in which he was engaged did not leave him the time necessary for an exhaustive search of the documents.

After this labor was done, Mr. J. W. S. Clements of Louisville, Kentucky, brought out his *Origins of the Clements-Spalding and Allied Families of Maryland and Kentucky,* whilst Mrs. Maria L. Kelley of Houston, Texas, issued her *Hamilton Family of Charles County, Maryland,* from which she is descended. Miss Mary Hallam of Washington, D. C., and Mr. Joseph W. Cambron of Louisville, Kentucky, kindly gave us the benefit of their studies on the Cambron family. Some items were also gleaned from the Hon. Benedict J. Webb's *Centenary of Catholicity in Kentucky.* Near kinsfolk (God bless them for their kindness) supplied us with a number of later facts and names which we could not have given otherwise.

Then, as a crippled condition combined with a lack of leisure to preclude all hope of further research, the matter gathered in these various ways was thrown into shape. The modest volume, while not without tedium and considerable difficulty, has been a labor of real pleasure. It could hardly have been otherwise, for Maryland has something of a sacred charm for those Catholics whose ancestors not only helped to plant the faith and the standard of religious toleration there, but also upheld both under severe tests. As Mr. Clements expresses the same idea in his charming little work mentioned above:

No power on earth can take from the Catholics the noble record of first planting the doctrine of religious tolerance among the sluggish streams and gentle hills of South Maryland. To have had forebears, no matter how humble, who helped in this famous work should be the source of extreme pride and satisfaction, only intensified by persecution endured for more than a hundred years. The Maryland Catholics anticipated the fathers of our republic on this question by almost a hundred and fifty years, and gave the first concrete example of the separation between church and state, now so vaunted, since the days of Constantine. Jefferson needed only to preach what he learned from early Maryland history.

For the reasons given above, and because of the lack and loss of documents, several gaps in the family lines have been necessarily left unfilled. Doubtless too, as in all works of the kind, there is an error here and there. But, under the circumstances, these defects could not be avoided by the writer. Yet it seemed well worth the while to have the result of his labors put in book form. The little volume will at least please those at whose behest it was written. Perhaps it may help some of them or their descendants.

The book is arranged in the form of five papers, the first two of which give the writer's ancestry on his father's side, while the other three show that on the part of his mother. These papers are followed by a summary of the lines of direct generation and a brief conclusion. For the sake of emphasis, or rather that they may serve as unmistakable guides, the names of the persons in the lines of our direct descent are put in *italics*. This method seemed at once the most natural and the easiest for the reader to follow. For the sake of brevity, as well as to save expense, in the mention of names we have limited ourself to the children of those in our direct lines and the issues of our immediate family. However, the blank pages at the end of the book, added for that purpose, can be used by all who may wish to fill out their own direct lines.

THE AUTHOR.

WASHINGTON, D. C.
FEBRUARY 22, 1933.

THE O'DANIELS AND THE O'BRIENS

The "O" and the apostrophe before the names O'Daniel and O'Brien leave no doubt as to their Irish origin. As a matter of fact, there is no patronymic better known, more numerous, or held in higher esteem in the Emerald Isle than that of O'Brien. Before the island's conquest by England those who bore it belonged to the country's nobility.

On the other hand, it is rare that one meets with the name O'Daniel in Irish history or annals. This lack of mention indicates that the O'Daniels were never very numerous in Ireland. Besides, we have been assured of this fact by several native scholars of the country. The earliest mention of the patronymic the writer has ever chanced upon was in a document in the archives of the Collegio Angelico, Rome. It is dated June 24, 1651, and tells of a Father Cornelius O'Daniel, an Irish Dominican, then in Saint Ann's Priory, Gratz, Styrian Austria.

There is a tradition in the family to the effect that the first O'Daniel in Maryland, whose descendants spread thence into Kentucky, came from around Cork, Ireland. It is quite possible that he was induced to come to America by Lord Baltimore himself, whose baronial estate lay in County Longford. One of Cecelius Calvert's principal aims in founding the Maryland Colony was to establish a home there for religious freedom. Quite naturally he was particularly anxious to enlist as many sturdy settlers of his own faith as he could in the noble enterprise, for the Catholics in the British Isles were then subject to all kinds of hardships and persecution. Doubtless, too, like many of the others, this early settler came to the New World in search of a place where he could practise his religion with safety.

The Ark and the Dove were the vessels which brought to Maryland the first pilgrims of religious toleration. They sailed from the Isle of Wight, off the southern coast of England, November 22, 1633, and reached Saint Clement's (now Blackiston) Island, in the southern part of the present State of Maryland, on March 25, 1634. Two days later, with the blessing of the Jesuit missionaries who accompanied them, they planted the banner of religious freedom and tolerance on the eastern bank of the Saint Mary's River, Saint Mary's County, and at once began plans for Saint Mary's City. The name of Saint Clement bestowed upon the island where they first halted, that of Saint Mary given to the river upon which they settled, the county which they began, and the incipient town, and the erection of a cross and the celebration of mass on the very day of their landing (the Feast of the Annunciation) all combined to give the enterprise a distinctly Catholic character and to place it under emphatically Catholic auspices. There is no more glorious page in the history of the Anglo-American colonies.[1]

---

[1] Maryland was the third English colony founded within the present United States, only Virginia and Massachusetts preceding it. Although established under Catholic auspices, Lord Baltimore and the government not merely tolerated all other Christian beliefs, but also invited their adherents to the palatinate. This rule prevailed until the Puritans gained the ascendancy. Then the Catholics were not only disfranchised, but even subjected to almost every kind of persecution. Indeed, from that time until the American Revolution Pennsylvania was the sole colony in which a Catholic enjoyed freedom. But there he could hold no public office.

It would be rash even to suggest that there might have been an O'Daniel in the original band of Maryland pioneers. However, the name appears on the records of the colony only a few years later. The Land Office at Annapolis shows a Thomas O'Daniel applying for a survey of land for himself and wife, "on the conditions of plantation," in 1663, less than two decades after the landing on Saint Mary's River. This document not merely proves that he had been in the province for some time; it also upholds the tradition among the O'Daniels of Kentucky that their American progenitors go back almost to the beginning of the Lord Baltimore Colony. The book of "Early Settlers" at Annapolis likewise gives his name. Besides, Thomas is a first or given name still found among the descendants of the O'Daniels who emigrated from Maryland to the Land of Bluegrass before the close of the first decade of the nineteenth century.

There is another family tradition which tells us that the forefathers of the O'Daniels who went out to Kentucky from the "Land of Sanctuary" lived on the "Eastern Shore," or the portion of Maryland which lies east of the Chesapeake Bay and the Susquehanna River. If this be true, as it apparently is, Thomas O'Daniel, or his immediate descendants, most likely moved to that part of the colony from Baltimore County, where he seems to have first settled. It is of record that he disposed of his original survey. In this connection, it should be noted that the well-known Catholic historian, John Gilmary Shea (page 368 of *The Catholic Church in Colonial Days*), is of the opinion that a number of Catholics changed their homes from the southern counties of Maryland to the northern stretches of the colony after the Puritans got into power and instituted a systematic persecution of those who belonged to the old faith. From there, in case of danger, Pennsylvania, where a more tolerant spirit prevailed, would be within easy reach.

By 1689, "Morris" (or Maurice) O'Daniel, probably a son of Thomas, had a landed estate in Cecil County (the extreme northeastern section of Maryland), between Elk River and the boundary of the present State of Delaware. It was known as "Morris O'Daniel's Rest." His will shows that his wife's first name was Marian. He had two daughters, called respectively Mary Ann and Margaret, and a brother named Daniel. The daughters, who did not marry, left their property to the Jesuit Fathers. It was afterwards incorporated in the possessions of those missionaries in Cecil County, which seem to have joined the estate of Augustine Herman known as "Bohemia Manor." There it was that the fathers, hampered by the spirit of the times, made their first serious attempt in Maryland to carry out their vocation of teaching, started a college, and began the education of the Most Rev. John Carroll, our proto-American bishop and archbishop.

The above bequest reveals the intimate relations which these pioneer O'Daniels cultivated with their spiritual directors, as well as their genuine Catholicity. A further manifestation of this religious character is found in the will of one Roger Sheehee. The document is dated April 25, and was probated June 12, 1674. Among the parties to whom the testator left personal property were included "the Roman Catholic Church" and "Love" (Charity) O'Daniel. Unfortunately the record does not tell in what part of the colony either Sheehee or Charity O'Daniel lived.[2]

It must be borne in mind that, for the reasons given in the foreword, want of time prevented the writer from making an exhaustive study of any of the family lines given in these papers. Thus the next mention of an O'Daniel in Maryland chanced upon, in the course of other researches, is that of a Richard O'Daniel, who was a soldier on the patriotic side in the American Revolution. He seems to have enlisted in Frederick County. The fact that he bore the same given name as the writer's father suggests a relationship. There is also a Michael O'Daniel shown in the 1790 census of Montgomery County. We know nothing more of either of these men.

Fortunately, beginning with the first of the patronymic who went out to Washington County, Kentucky, the traditions are so clear and exact that they leave little or no room for doubt about their truth in the main. We drank them in from childhood. From 1830, the date of the earliest extant records at Saint Rose's, near Springfield, they are upheld in ever so many instances by church entries. The county registers also often sustain them. We remember two of these early Kentucky O'Daniels, Walter and James, for they lived to be very old men.

About the end of the American Revolution, an attractive Irish girl by the name of *Mary O'Brien* came from Cork to Cecil County, Maryland. There she soon

---

[2] See *The Maryland Calendar of Wills*, I, 82.

married *Joseph O'Daniel,* whom tradition represents as having been a soldier on our side in the War of Independence. We can not suppress the idea that he was a son or brother of a James "O'Danald" (O'Daniel), who lived near Warwick, in the southeastern part of Cecil County, for that given name is still not uncommon among the Kentucky O'Daniels. It is worthy of note that from at least 1794 to 1799 this James O'Daniel was an overseer or manager of land belonging to the Jesuit Fathers, for it is a further proof of the religious spirit of those who bore the patronymic. In any case, sometime in the first decade of the nineteenth century, attracted by the reports of the great fertility and cheapness of the soil in the new country, *Joseph* set out for Kentucky with his wife, three sons, and five daughters. Like the greater number of the early seekers of homes in the west, they travelled in covered wagons, carrying along with them whatever household and farm utensils might be of immediate necessity when they reached their destination.

The wayfarers, possibly to save expense, took the more southerly route followed by many of the pioneers across Virginia to the Cumberland Gap. When almost through this break in the mountains, *Joseph O'Daniel, Sr.,* returned to a blacksmith shop, which they had passed only a short distance, in order to have something made. He told his family to continue their way, for he would soon overtake them. As he did not return as soon as they expected, they decided to wait for him. Two days or more thus went by. His son *Joseph* and a colored man were then sent in search of him. To their horror they learned that he had been seized and taken into the mountains by highwaymen, who then slew him and made away with the money he had on his person and the fine horse he rode. In those days it was not an uncommon thing for such a catastrophe to befall single travellers or small bands bound for the west while they were in the fastnesses of the Cumberland Gap.

Stunned, but undaunted, by the loss of her beloved husband, *Mrs. O'Daniel* continued her way with the rest of the family. The tradition which represents her as a woman of rare courage must be true. She located near the southern end of the Catholic settlement on Cartwright's Creek. The farm she secured lay just a little to the west of the stream itself. In his youth the writer often saw the place, for his own home was not far distant. Just when she reached Kentucky we can not say; but the federal census of 1810, the earliest extant for the state, shows her in Washington County then with her three sons and five daughters. Doubtless because of the phonetic spelling of the census-taker, which is often found in our early documents, the name is written O'Danald, just as is that of James O'Daniel of Cecil County, Maryland, mentioned above.[3]

Through her good management and the industry of her children *Mrs. Mary O'Daniel* prospered in her new home. However, she did not remain a widow. In 1818, two years after the marriage of her eldest son, *Joseph,* she became the wife of "Mathers" (Matthew) Doyle, a widower who had himself gone out to Kentucky from

---

[3] Even today a stranger, hearing the name pronounced in the slurring way common in Kentucky, would write it Erdanel, Erdanald, Danel, or Danald rather than O'Daniel.

Maryland. She then disposed of her farm to *Joseph O'Daniel, Jr.,* and went to live with her husband on that which he owned. The former Matthew Doyle homestead we have also often seen—passed it, in fact, every time we went to church and for some years on our way to and from school; but the buildings on it had disappeared before the days of our recollection. They stood on the part of the farm of the sons of the late "Wat" (Walter) O'Bryan which was recently purchased by Mrs. Annie Vise.

The records of Saint Rose's Church show that Matthew Doyle was buried on March 25, 1835. They also tell us that *"Mrs. Mary Doyle* [was buried] August 14, 1859—aged ninety-two years." This fact places her birth in 1767. More than one of her great-grandchildren were practically grown before her death. From these, her grandchildren (the writer's father among them), and other old persons have we learned that she was a charming character; that she retained a clear mind and memory until the end; that she was born in Cork, Ireland; that she came to America as a young woman; that she married *Joseph O'Daniel* on the "Eastern Shore," or in Cecil County, Maryland; and that her first husband fought in the American Revolution. After Mr. Doyle's death, she went to live with her son *Joseph,* the writer's grandfather, and placed her youngest son, James, on the Doyle farm, which was left to her by will during her natural lifetime. *Joseph O'Daniel,* we have been told countless times, took a keen delight in getting his mother, in her vigorous old age, to sing Irish songs and dance Irish jigs. These interesting performances afforded her no less pleasure than the others derived from them.[4]

Joseph, the eldest son of *Joseph* and *Mary (O'Brien) O'Daniel,* married *Nancy,* the daughter of *William* and *Rebecca (Montgomery) Cambron,* who lived in the adjoining neighborhood. This was in 1816. The next paper will tell of these two families—the Cambrons and the Montgomerys. Saint Rose's Church, built by Fathers Edward Dominic Fenwick (afterwards the first bishop of Cincinnati) and Samuel Thomas Wilson in 1808 and 1809, stood some two miles west of Springfield. The Cambrons and O'Daniels lived in this parish. Thus, although the extant parish records do not go back earlier than 1830, it is certain that *Joseph* and *Nancy (Cambron) O'Daniel* were joined in wedlock by some Dominican Father at Saint Rose's. Tradition tells us that Father Samuel T. Wilson, a provincial of holy memory and a light of the early Church in Kentucky, performed the ceremony; and the tradition is borne out by the fact that several Cambron children were named after the great English divine, whom, like every one else, the family greatly admired.

Joseph and *Nancy (Cambron) O'Daniel* were blessed with six sons and two daughters who attained mature manhood and womanhood. The marble slab

---

[4] From early youth and almost times without number have we heard the facts recorded in the last six paragraphs. The longevity of *Mrs. Mary (O'Brien-O'Daniel) Doyle,* of course, was responsible for the preservation of the greater number of them. Her second husband, who was a man of some note, is said to have been universally called "Matthers" Doyle; and his first name is so written in the record of his funeral at Saint Rose's. Their marriage license at Springfield shows that it was Matthew.

which fortunately still marks *Mrs. O'Daniel's* grave at Saint Rose's shows that she was born December 24, 1796, and died March 5, 1857. Accordingly she was past sixty years of age at the time of her death. *Joseph O'Daniel* died of pneumonia February 13, 1864. His tombstone, in a different part of the same cemetery, tells us that he was born September 1, 1792. Thus he was in his seventy-second year when he departed this life. They were splendid Catholics, good neighbors, and among the most highly respected members of the extensive parish of Saint Rose. Because of their model lives they left a memory that was long cherished. Hubert Mattingly now owns and lives on the central part of their old homestead, which long since passed out of the hands of their family.

Richard Jefferson, commonly called *"Jeff,"* was the fourth son and sixth child of *Joseph* and *Nancy (Cambron) O'Daniel.* He was married twice. His first wife was Sarah Ann, daughter of George and Lucinda (Spalding) Melton, who lived in the Poplar Neck Settlement, Nelson County, Kentucky. The marriage ceremony was performed by Father Charles Truyens, S.J., of Bardstown, September 6, 1856. The stone marking her grave at Saint Rose's says she was born May 6, 1841, and died March 9, 1858. This confirms what the writer has always heard—that she was a mere child. To this union was born Georgia Ann O'Daniel, who lived only six years. The little marble slab which used to stand at the head of her grave, but has lately disappeared, gave August 12, 1857, as the date of her birth, and August 25, 1863, as that of her death.⁵

Meanwhile *Richard J.*, or *"Jeff,"* *O'Daniel* had married again, taking as his second wife *Sarah Ann,* always called *Nancy,* daughter of *William Thompson* and *Lucy (Edelen) Hamilton.*⁶ This troth was plighted in Saint Charles' Church, Marion County, Kentucky, February 14, 1860, the Rev. Francis De Muelder officiating. The home of *Richard J.* and *Sarah Ann,* or *Nancy, (Hamilton) O'Daniel* was on the present Saint Rose-Lebanon Turnpike, about half way between the two places. There they both died; there all their children and some of their grandchildren were born. It had been *Jeff O'Daniel's* home before his second marriage. The farm lay on both sides of a little stream called Shepherd's Run, and was not far from where lived his father, *Joseph O'Daniel.* In the division of Washington County (1834 or 1835), the lower part of which was taken to form that of Marion, this homestead was left just inside Washington County. But in 1869 (the year after the writer's birth), when the line between the two counties was straightened, it was thrown into Marion. One half of the place is today owned by Richard Osbourn, and the other by Alex (Joseph Alexander) Osbourn. The house was destroyed by fire about thirty years ago.

---

⁵ The dates of Mrs. O'Daniel's funeral and that of Georgia Ann, together with the latter's baptism, are also given in the records at Saint Rose's. Ever so many of the tombstones in the graveyard there have disappeared within the past quarter of a century. Often has the writer seen those of Matthew and *Mary* [*O'Brien-O'Daniel*] Doyle; but they exist no longer. The dates of the births of himself, his second wife, and his children, together with the dates of the deaths of those who died young, are given in the handwriting (in a little book) of R. J. O'Daniel himself.

⁶ Thompson was one of *Mr. Hamilton's* first names.

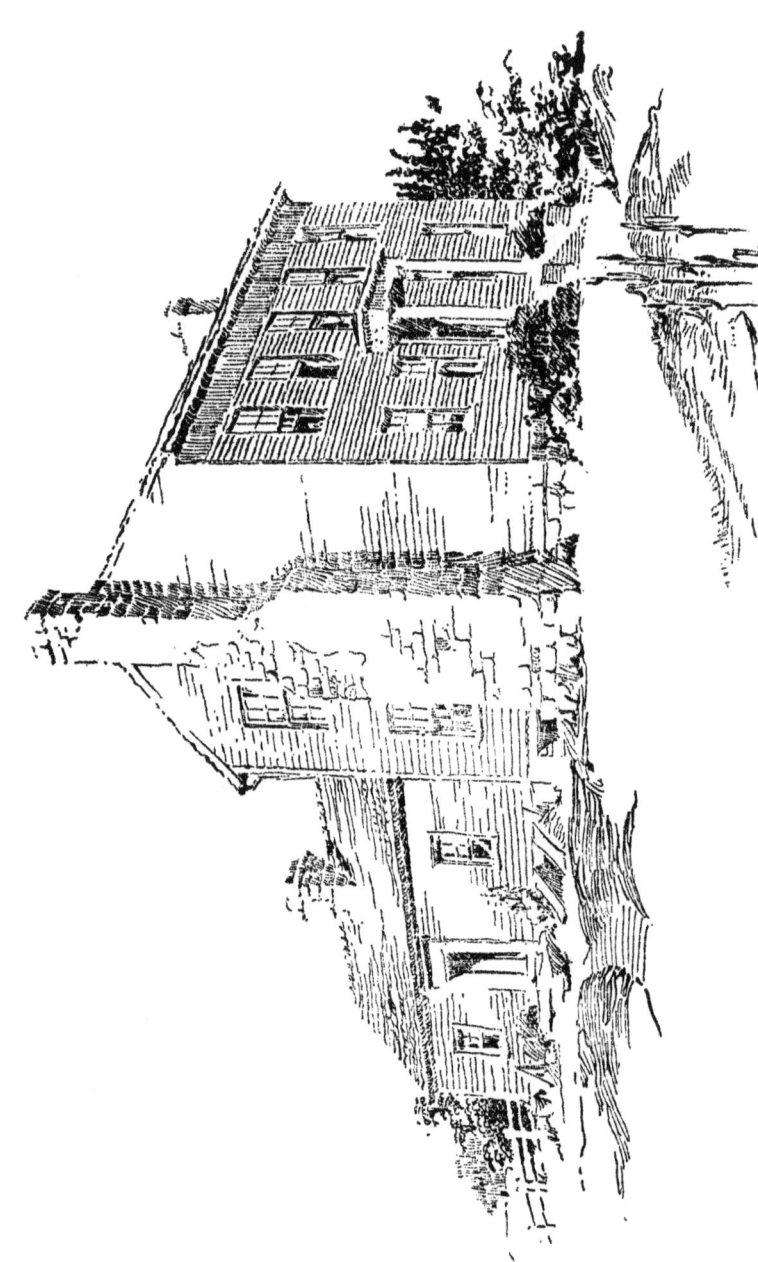

THE FORMER HOME OF MR. AND MRS. R. J. O'DANIEL

As a matter of family history, it may be noted that *R. J. O'Daniel's* homestead seems certainly to have been a part of that of *William Cambron,* his maternal grandfather. At any rate, it had certainly been owned by Cambrons. In fact, so many of that family name had lived in the vicinity that, as stated in the foreword, it was long known as "the Cambron neighborhood." Just south of it, towards Lebanon, now in Marion County, lay what was called "the Hamilton neighborhood." It extended from the present Lebanon-Springfield Turnpike, or Highway, westward to Hardin's Creek. In this latter stretch of country, about a mile and a half from where she ended her earthly career, was born and reared *Sarah Ann Hamilton,* or the second *Mrs. O'Daniel.* The home of her parents, *William T.* and *Lucy (Edelen) Hamilton,* was long a "station" of Saint Charles' Parish, where the priest was ever warmly welcomed to say mass for the aged and infirm or to baptize the children of that vicinity. The part of the plantation on which their house stood has recently passed into the hands of Roger Parrott.

Jeff, or *Richard J., O'Daniel* first saw the light of day February 2, 1831. Evidently distance from the church, ugly weather, and bad roads caused his baptism to be somewhat delayed, for the records at Saint Rose's show that this sacred ceremony was performed upon him by the revered Father Joseph Thomas Jarboe, O.P., on March 27 of that year. He died July 28, 1900. His second wife, *Sarah Ann,* or *Nancy (Hamilton) O'Daniel,* was born March 24, 1833, and was baptized at Saint Charles' by the Rev. David Deparcq. She died August 2, 1893. Possibly because it was the church of her girlhood she and her husband often attended Saint Charles' Church during the early years of their married life; and it was there, or at the former "station" of the *William T. Hamilton* homestead, that their first four children were baptized. The other five received that sacrament at Saint Rose's.[7] Better Christians never lived than *Richard J.* and *Sarah Ann (Hamilton) O'Daniel*. Not merely did they have many friends; they were admired and beloved by all who knew them. To the writer's personal knowledge their funerals were attended by exceptionally large crowds —their deaths bemoaned far and wide. The poor, especially the colored people, felt that they had lost benefactors on whom they could ever rely. All this was a tribute of genuine worth. Their bodies lie side by side, awaiting the day of resurrection, in the graveyard of Saint Rose's, which is hallowed by many sacred memories.

God blessed this model couple with a large family, two of whom died in their infancy. One became a Dominican Father, and two Dominican Sisters. Four married. Their names; the dates of their births, together with the dates of the deaths of those who are no longer with us; the husband of the one daughter and the wives of the three sons who married; and their children will be given in the lists that are to follow.

By way of conclusion it may be noted that there are a number of O'Daniels scattered here and there through the State of Kentucky, whose ancestors went there from

---

[7] We confirmed the family tradition about these baptisms by the records at Saint Charles' and Saint Rose's. Unfortunately, as we understand, those of the former church have been since destroyed by fire.

Maryland at an early date. In Grayson County, for instance, we are told there are several of the patronymic; and the first names among them suggest descent from the same stock as those of whom we have written. Probably they are descended from a John O'Daniel we found in Nelson County as early as 1794. However, want of time and a crippled condition did not permit us to attempt to trace their lineage. While in search of other historical data, we came across persons by the name of Daniel in the former Lord Baltimore Colony, whose associations indicated that they were Irish. We wondered if, for some reason or other, they did not drop the prefix "O" from their names. Such things have been done frequently enough. There were also a few O'Daniels in Virginia and North Carolina in the early days. Their descendants can hardly be of the faith, for there were then no priests in those two states. The lists of soldiers in the American Revolution show men of the name fighting in the cause of liberty in Massachusetts and New Jersey. We know nothing more of them. However, we should not be surprised if they really belonged to Maryland, whose military records of the time were not well kept.

O'DANIEL LIST I

Joseph O'Daniel, born in Maryland (most likely in Cecil County), died in the Cumberland Gap, Kentucky; and

Mary (O'Brien) O'Daniel, born in Cork, Ireland, in 1767, died in Kentucky, in 1835.

THEIR CHILDREN:—

Ruth—married Matthew Carrico.
Joseph—married *Nancy Cambron.*
Elizabeth—married Joseph Molohon.
James—married Mary Cambron.
Sally (or Sarah)—married Benedict Cambron.
Walter—married (1st) Nancy Cambron; (2ndly) Susan Wheatley.
Hettie—married Raymond Montgomery.
Mary—married Raphael Cambron.

We have placed these O'Daniels in the chronological order of their marriages as shown in the records at Springfield. That of their births was very likely somewhat different. It will be remembered that they were all born in Maryland and brought to Kentucky in their youth. The wives of *Joseph* and James and the husband of Sally (or Sarah) were children of *William* and *Rebecca (Montgomery) Cambron;* the first wife of Walter a daughter of John Basil and Lucy (Smith) Cambron; and the husband of Mary a son of Henry and Margaret (Harbin) Cambron. We do not know who were the parents of Ruth's and Elizabeth's husbands. Walter's second wife was a daughter of James and Susan (Riney) Wheatley. *William,* Henry, and John Basil Cambron were sons of *Baptist,* or rather *John Baptist,* Cambron, of whom we shall tell in the next paper.

Joseph and *Nancy (Cambron) O'Daniel* (as already stated), Matthew and Ruth (O'Daniel) Carrico, and Raymond and Hettie (O'Daniel) Montgomery are buried at Saint Rose's. Joseph and Elizabeth

(O'Daniel) Molohon, we think, are buried at Raywick, Kentucky. Benedict Cambron is buried at Saint Rose's, but we are of the opinion that his wife, Sally (O'Daniel) Cambron, is buried in the adjoining parish of Saint Charles. Walter and Nancy (Cambron) O'Daniel are also buried at Saint Charles', while his second wife was laid to rest in the graveyard at Chicago, Kentucky. Raphael and Mary (O'Daniel) Cambron are buried in the cemetery of Sacred Heart Church, Union County, Kentucky. James and Mary (Cambron) O'Daniel moved to Monroe County, Missouri, shortly after 1855; but they returned to Kentucky in their old age. Their mortal remains repose side by side in the graveyard at Saint Rose's. The writer remembers them well in their last years.

O'DANIEL LIST II

Joseph O'Daniel (2nd), born in Maryland, possibly Cecil County, September 1, 1792, died in Kentucky February 13, 1864; and
Nancy (Cambron) O'Daniel, born in Washington County, Kentucky, December 24, 1796, died there March 5, 1857.

THEIR CHILDREN:—
1. James—married Martina Wheatley.
2. Edward—married Mary R. Spalding.
3. Cassie—married James Spalding.
4. Josiah—married Josephine Mullican.
5. Rose—married Richard Hamilton.
6. *Richard Jefferson*—married (1st) Sarah Ann of George and Lucinda (Spalding) Melton;

(2ndly) *Sarah Ann* of *William T.* and *Lucy (Edelen) Hamilton.*
7. Christopher—died single.
8. Pius—married (1st) Anna Head — no issue; (2ndly) Cornelia Thompson.

Edward's wife and Cassie's husband were children of Peter and Sarah (Walker) Spalding of the Poplar Neck Settlement, Nelson County. *Richard J's* first wife was a granddaughter of the same Peter and Sarah Spalding. Josiah's wife was a daughter of John ("Jack") and Susan (Hayden) Mullican, who also lived in the Poplar Neck Settlement. Rose's husband was a son of Hoskins and Eliza (Clements) Hamilton, who lived near Lebanon, and a grandson of the Thomas Hamilton to be mentioned in the paper on the Hamiltons. James' wife was a daughter of James and Susan (Riney) Wheatley. We do not know who were the parents of Pius' two wives. James is buried at Saint Rose's, near his mother, and his wife in another part of the same cemetery. Edward and his wife are buried at Saint Charles'—Christopher at Raywick. Rose and her husband are buried in Louisville—Cassie and her husband at Chicago, Kentucky. Josiah and his wife were laid to rest in Owensboro. Pius' first wife is buried at Raywick, whilst his own mortal remains and those of his second wife repose in Louisville. *Richard J.* and his two wives, as already stated, await the day of resurrection in the graveyard of Saint Rose's. We knew all these people except James, Richard's first wife, and Pius' second.

R. J. O'DANIEL, AT THE AGE OF SEVENTY YEARS

MRS. R. J. O'DANIEL, THE SECOND, WHEN YOUNG

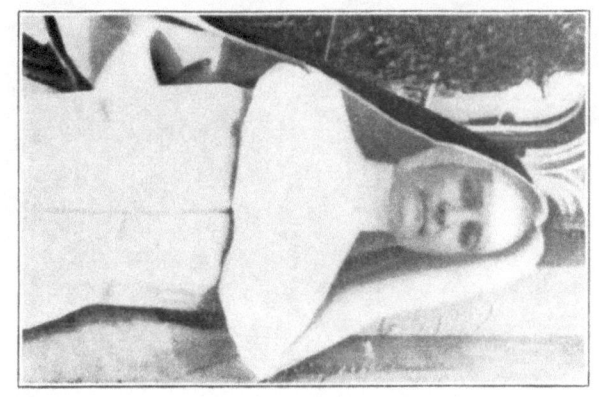

SISTER FRANCESCA O'DANIEL

SITTING, LEFT TO RIGHT: MRS. LOU (O'DANIEL) MULLICAN, SISTER ROSALIA O'DANIEL
STANDING, LEFT TO RIGHT: L. E., REV. V. F. T. J. AND W. J. O'DANIEL

O'DANIEL LIST III

Richard J., or *"Jeff," O'Daniel,* born in Washington, now Marion, County, Kentucky, February 2, 1831, died in the latter county, July 28, 1900; and

Sarah Ann, or *Nancy (Hamilton) O'Daniel,* born in Washington, now Marion, County, Kentucky, March 24, 1833, died in the latter county, August 2, 1893.

THEIR CHILDREN:—

1. Anna Lucy (called Lou)—born November 19, 1860; married Lloyd T. Mullican of Daviess County, and son of John (Jack) and Susan (Hayden) Mullican.
2. William Joseph—born June 8, 1862; married Mary Ellen of Richard and Emily Jane (Brady) Cummins, and widow of Thomas Abell of Lebanon.
3. John M.—born February 9, 1864; died March 7, 1865.
4. Thomas Jefferson ("Jeff")—born March 19, 1866; married (1st) Hettie of John Dallas and Susan C. (Abell) Simms, and (2ndly) Annie of Joseph H. and Elizabeth Ann (Beaven) Hagan—both of Marion County.
5. Victor Francis—born February 15, 1868; a Dominican priest.
6. Francis L.—born October 15, 1869, died February 2, 1870.
7. Edward Lawrence (called Lawrence)—born December 17, 1870; married Osie of Francis

and Mary Elizabeth (Lydan) Kelly—Washington County.

8. Mary Rose (Sister Rosalia, O.S.D.)—born January 3, 1873, died at Saint Catherine's Academy, near Springfield, Kentucky, March 26, 1921.
9. Ida Mary (Sister Francesca, O.S.D.)—born June 23, 1875, died at the Academy of Saint Mary's of the Springs, Columbus, Ohio, July 9, 1901.

O'DANIEL LIST IV

Anna Lucy, or Lou, O'Daniel, as above; and Lloyd T. Mullican, as above. He was born April 3, 1853, and died January 29, 1913—buried at **Stanley, Daviess County, Kentucky.**

THEIR CHILDREN:—

1. Nannie—born, during a visit of her mother, at her grandfather O'Daniel's; married Richard L. of George Thomas and Mary Ann, or "Maranda Jane," (Monarch-Hagan) O'Bryan.
2. William—born in Daviess County; married Eva of Charles and Susan Marie (Mattingly) Lancaster.
3. Catherine, or "Katie,"— born in Daviess County; married Benedict of Miles Nicholas and Ruth (Kelley) Lancaster. He was born September 26, 1886, and died April 29, 1925 —buried in Owensboro.

4. Clara—born in Daviess County; married Thomas of Charles and Susan Marie (Mattingly) Lancaster.
5. Ella—born in Daviess County; married Victor of Armstead and Annie Elizabeth (Kelley) Servant.

Thomas and Eva Lancaster are brother and sister. Benedict Lancaster was their first cousin. Ella Mullican married out of her Church; and, as far as we know, is still out of it. All these people belong to Daviess County.

O'DANIEL LIST V

Thomas Jefferson ("Jeff") O'Daniel—born as in O'Daniel List III, and Hettie Simms, his first wife.

THEIR CHILDREN:—

1. Nannie—born at the home of her grandfather O'Daniel; married Joseph of Archibald S. and Mary (Douglass) O'Daniel, of Marion County.
2. Joseph—born at the home of his grandfather O'Daniel; married Elizabeth of Joseph and Emma Josephine (Shader) Spalding, of Springfield.
3. John Dallas—born at the home of his grandfather O'Daniel; married Minnie of George W. and Lucy C. (Brown) Padfield, of Nashville, Illinois.

Thomas Jefferson ("Jeff") O'Daniel and Annie Hagan, his second wife.

THEIR CHILDREN:—

1. Raymond—born in Marion County.
2. Richard—born in Marion County; married Effie Elizabeth of Adison Nuel and Catherine Belle (Stetz) Scribner, of Louisville.

Hettie Simms, "Jeff" O'Daniel's first wife, was born May 9, 1873, and died June 17, 1903. "Jeff" himself died November 3, 1928. Both buried in Lebanon.

O'DANIEL LIST VI

Edward Lawrence, or Lawrence, O'Daniel—born as in O'Daniel List III; and Osie Kelly.

THEIR CHILDREN:—

1. Francis—born at the home of his grandfather O'Daniel; married Mary Rose of John Michael and Harriet Ann (Johnson) Cooper, of Lebanon.
2. Louise—born in Marion County; married Joseph of John Henry and Frances (Padgett) Bryan, of Louisville.
3. Ida—born in Marion County; married Richard of Richard and Annie (Blandford) Osbourn, of Washington County.
4. Margaret—born in Marion County; married Arthur of William and Mary Genevieve (Smith) Clayton, of same county.

THE O'DANIELS AND O'BRIENS   33

5. Elizabeth—born in Marion County; married Henry, or "Harry," of Charles H. and Mary Ellen (Hayden) Jarboe, of Louisville.
6. William—born in Marion County; married Elizabeth of Francis Guy and Mary Dorothy (Rapier) Combs, of Louisville.
7. Victor Francis — born in Marion County; married Bessie Lee of W. Garvie and Jennie (Hocker) Nelson, of Louisville.
8. Cecilia—born in Marion County.
9. Osie—born in Marion County.

There was no issue from the marriage of William Joseph and Mary Ellen (Cummins-Abell) O'Daniel; and for this reason there was no list to be made for them. However, Mrs. O'Daniel had a daughter, Alma, by her first husband, Thomas Abell. Alma married Lee Goodin of Lebanon, and they have a nice young family. Mrs. Mary Ellen (Cummins-Abell) O'Daniel was born at Raywick, Kentucky, July 30, 1865, and died in Lebanon February 16, 1931. Buried in Lebanon.

Like those of practically all the pioneer Catholics of the Cartwright's Creek Settlement, Washington and Marion counties, Kentucky, the descendants of *Joseph* and *Mary (O'Brien) O'Daniel* are scattered in many places west of the Alleghany Mountains. This is especially true of those descended from their son James, who had a very large family and moved to Missouri. Some are in the east. But the greater number seem to be still in Kentucky. However, no one of that family name now resides in the original parish limits of Saint Rose's. Everywhere they have been, and still are, notably true to the Catholic faith. Numbers of the female descendants of *Joseph and Mary (O'Brien) O'Daniel* have joined our various Catholic sisterhoods. Yet, despite their religious loyalty, only two, in so far as we know, have become priests. One of these is Father Victor F. O'Daniel, O.P., mentioned in **O'Daniel List III**. The other is Father Joseph V. Somes of the Diocese of Indianapolis, whose mother is a daughter of Josiah and Josephine (Mullican) O'Daniel noted in **O'Daniel List II**.

THE CAMBRONS AND THE MONTGOMERYS

The name Cambron goes back almost to the dawn of Scottish history. In the early days, when spelling was a neglected art, we find it written in ever so many ways—Cambron, Cambrun, Cameron, Camron, Camrun, Chambron, and otherwise.[1] During the period of French influence in the British Isles it was sometimes preceded by the Gallic particle "De". The clan was long one of the most powerful in Scotland. They belonged to the country's nobility. In the course of time, though no older than some of the others, Cameron became the more common spelling of the name; and it is now the one by which the clan, as a rule, is known everywhere.

A family tradition, so strong, distinct, and persistent that we can not doubt it, tells us that the first Cambron in Maryland came from Scotland itself; that he was not brought up in the Catholic faith; and that he entered the Church after his arrival in America. The traditional story of his conversion is too interesting to be omitted. Six Cameron brothers (or, as some say, seven) came to Maryland. They had been reared Presbyterians. One of them married a Catholic lady in the Lord Baltimore Colony, and then he embraced her religion. It was a brave act in the Maryland of that time, for religious intolerance was at high tide. The other five brothers were so incensed at his conversion

---

[1] Some of these various spellings were no doubt due to clerks, who wrote the name phonetically, or as it sounded to them because of a slurring pronunciation.

that they disowned him. As a result of the family discord the new convert changed the "e" in his name to "b." In other words, he resumed one of the old spellings of the patronymic, and called himself Cambron, the name which his descendants have retained, together with a staunch fidelity to Catholicity.

We remember well a journey of the Benedict Cambron mentioned in the foreword and Thomas O'Bryan (the latter still living) to Missouri in the fall of 1877. They went there with a view of settling in that state, provided the prospects suited them. Time and again Mr. Cambron told us that in Cameron City, Clinton County, where they stopped at a hotel, a pleasant sort of man, who appeared to be the innkeeper, accosted him somewhat after this fashion: "I see your name is Cambron. From that I conclude you are from either Maryland or Kentucky; that you are a Catholic; and that I can claim a distant relationship with you, although I am a Presbyterian." The disciple of John Knox then proceeded to tell the Catholic traveller from Kentucky the story which we have just related. Mr. Cameron knew that a number of Cambrons had gone out from Maryland to Kentucky in the pioneer days, and wondered if the tradition still lived among their descendants there. He seemed greatly pleased to learn that it did, and showed Benedict Cambron no little kindness.[2] This fact seems to be a conclusive proof of the truth of the

---

[2] It is history that nearly all Scotland, largely through the influence of John Knox, became Presbyterian. Some of the Camerons, or Cambrons, however, remained true to the old faith. Several of the name even fled to the Continent in order to escape persecution or death. Cameron City, Missouri, was given that name by one of its founders, Samuel McCorkle, in honor of his wife's father, who was a Cameron.

THE CAMBRONS AND MONTGOMERYS 37

tradition. The traditions of long-standing in Kentucky generally have a good kernel of truth in them.

The earliest mention of a Cambron, or any Camerons, we found in the records of Maryland during our researches was in the first half of the eighteenth century. There was a Finley Cameron and a John Cameron among the Scotsmen made prisoners and sent over to Maryland as exiles by the English after the defeat of the brave Highlanders in the Battle of Preston. That was in 1716 and 1717. Others fled from their country to "the Land of Sanctuary" for safety's sake. Thus a little later we find an Anthony Cameron in the colony. Similarly, Liber 29 (folio 478) of Testamentary Proceedings at Annapolis shows a John Andrew "Camburn" in Saint Mary's County going security for the bond of an administratrix in Charles County in December, 1734. We are inclined to think that he also lived in the latter county. At any rate, an account of the lord proprietor's Manor of Zacchia in Charles County gives an Andrew "Cambrun" as a lessee on that estate in 1746. The spelling "Camburn" and "Cambrun," we take it for granted, was the phonetic work of the clerk in the first instance and of the bookkeeper in the second. That was a very, very common occurrence in the distant past; nay, it is still done from time to time. Andrew and John Andrew seem certainly to have been the same person. No doubt the above men were four of the six brothers mentioned in the tradition of which we have told. Most likely too Andrew Cambron was the Catholic convert whose descendants emigrated from Charles County, Maryland, to Kentucky. He fits in nicely with the time they went west.

Be this as it may, the people of Charles County were among the most enthusiastic in Maryland in favor of the American Revolution; nor were the Cambrons the least loyal of the patriots there. Folio 639 of Liber X (10), in the registry of deeds office at La Plata, gives *Baptist* (that is, *John Baptist*), Henry, James, Milbron (or Milbern), and Thomas Cambron among those who took the Oath of Fidelity to the American cause. Although we did not discover it, others add James M. Cambron, which was likely the full name of Milbron, or Milbern. They all belonged to the Bryantown Hundred, or district, Charles County. *Baptist* (or *John Baptist*) was Henry's father. The rest were most likely brothers or near relatives of the older man. *Baptist's* other sons were too young to take the oath, the age designated for it being from eighteen to fifty years.

John Baptist Cambron, whose first name is generally abbreviated to *Baptist,* went to Kentucky with his ten children, seven sons and three daughters, in 1788 or 1789. He was then a widower. Who his wife was we do not know; but the family tradition that her first name was Nancy is borne out by the number of his early female descendants who were similarly called. It is tradition, and almost certain, that he went west direct from Charles County, Maryland. The fact that the Cambrons took the Oath of Fidelity in that county shows that it was their home. Mr. Webb's statement *(op. cit.,* page 69) that he went from Montgomery County is contradicted by the records of that county, for they nowhere mention the name Cambron. The assertion of the same author that *Baptist's* son Henry took him to Kentucky is refuted by the fact that the entire large family accompanied him thither. This was evidently the work of a father, not that of a son. It seems quite certain that he moved westward for the temporal advantage of his children and to obtain land which had been awarded him for services in the Revolutionary war.[3]

The farm which *John Baptist Cambron* procured lay almost in the middle of the Cartwright's Creek Settlement, Washington County, Kentucky, and about two miles nearly due west from the present Saint Rose's Church and Priory. The Saint Rose-Loretto Turnpike now passes the place. A good Christian man, he took a keen interest in the affairs of his religion, and was one of the first to start that Catholic settlement. No doubt his activity in such matters had its part in the erection of Saint Ann's, a small log church which rose in the immediate vicinity of his new home a few years after he settled there. In the boyhood days of the writer a walled fountain not more than a quarter of a mile from where Saint Ann's had stood was known as the "Baptist Cambron spring." It is still so called by the older people at least. Evidently it supplied the family with drinking water. Near it stands a chimney, with the date 1810 carved on one of the stones, which no doubt belonged to an addition to the original house, or perhaps to a second and more pretentious dwelling erected by the old soldier. In the boyhood and young manhood

---

[3] The family tradition that he was a soldier in the Revolutionary War is persistent; and it is corroborated by his Oath of Fidelity and the brief sketch of the life of his grandson, John Baptist Cambron, the second, on pages 66 and 67 of the *History of Union County, Kentucky*. Mr. Webb got his two erroneous opinions from page 71 of the Rev. Camillus P. Maes' *Life of Rev. Charles Nerinckx.*

of the writer that part of his farm belonged to Robert Montgomery. It is now owned by Oscar Graves.

The pioneer Catholic settler did not live long after the date carved on the chimney mentioned above. His will is dated May 23, 1814; and it was probated May 8, 1815. A family tradition still tells us that he was laid to rest in the little graveyard which surrounded the log Saint Ann's. The graves have no tombstones, for they were then a prohibitive luxury in the backwoods of Kentucky, or mayhap could not even be had for love or money. Saint Ann's ceased to be used in 1819, Saint Rose's having practically supplanted it ten years earlier. But *Baptist,* or *John Baptist, Cambron* doubtless preferred the God's acre around the humble house of prayer which he had helped to raise with his own hands, and which was almost at the door of his own home.

While many of them are scattered far and wide, perhaps none of the pioneer Catholic settlers of Kentucky are today represented by a greater number of descendants in the state than *Baptist Cambron.* Hosts of them still live in Marion, Washington, and Nelson counties. Not a few are in Louisville. Although not ordinarily blessed with much wealth, they are people of the highest respectability. What is more, the posterity of none of the planters of the faith in the Land of Blue Grass have adhered more steadfastly to their religion. That *Baptist,* who seems to have lived to a great age, was an influential and outstanding character in his day is evidenced by the fact that no name in the Cartwright's Creek Settlement has been better preserved there. It has been handed down from generation to generation. It is known and held in high esteem by everybody.

Even those of his line who live in distant parts know about him, and feel proud in being able to claim him as an ancestor.

The names of *John Baptist Cambron's* children will be given in the list which is to follow. But here we may note that Horace, after whom several of the venerable patriarch's descendants were named, did not remain long in Washington County. Stephen, who married late in life, spent many years in Nelson County, but returned to that of Washington towards the end of his life. Thomas is said to have moved to Grayson County with his family after 1820. The others remained in the parish of Saint Rose, in whose graveyard they and their husbands or wives are buried. Henry married in Maryland. The absence of any record of their marriage licenses at Bardstown or Springfield indicates that some of the others had also found life-partners before they went west. Tradition tells us that a brother of *Baptist* moved to Kentucky about the same time as he did; and in the 1810 federal census of Washington County we find a James Cambron, a Leonard Cambron, a Samuel Cambron, two by the name of Ignatius, and two by the name of John, while the Nelson County census for the same year shows a James M. Cambron. All these were doubtless blood relations of the old Trojan *Baptist*. However we did not try to trace them, for they belonged to side lines.[4]

William Montgomery and his wife **Ann** are the first

---

[4] Our purpose is to give merely the direct line of descent of our own family from *John Baptist Cambron.* Doubtless because of the slurring pronunciation referred to in note 1, the name is written (by clerks) in various ways in the early Washington County records.

of that family name we discovered in the records of Maryland. They appear as witnesses to the will of one John Wheeler of Charles County in 1693. Just how long they had been in the colony we can not say. It is certain that they were Catholics, and quite probable that they were the progenitors of the many later Montgomerys in the same county, all of whom were highly respected citizens as well as staunch in the faith. They were among the county's most patriotic citizens at the time of the American Revolution. Several of them served in that war; and no less than ten of them took the Oath of Fidelity to the sacred cause. They seem to have been about equally divided between the Port Tobacco and Bryantown hundreds or districts. Some from both of these localities joined in the early Catholic exodus from Maryland to Kentucky, and secured homes in the Cartwright's Creek Settlement. There they soon became leaders in civil affairs as well as in those of their religion.[5]

Among the people of Charles County shown in the 1790 federal census (the first taken) is a Widow *Henrietta Montgomery*. All indications point to the Bryantown section as that in which she lived. Her husband, *John,* appears to have been killed, or died, as a soldier in the Revolutionary War; and she seems to have been the daughter of one Ignatius Jenkins of Baltimore

---

[5] We have seen it stated that some of the early Montgomerys in the Cartwright's Creek Settlement went there from Montgomery County, Maryland. But this is against tradition. Besides, the records of Charles County show that it was the home of the Maryland Catholic Montgomerys. Neither the records of Montgomery nor those of Frederick County, from which Montgomery was taken in 1776, show the names of any of the early Montgomerys in the Cartwright's Creek Settlement.

THE CAMBRONS AND MONTGOMERYS

County. She had two single daughters. Two sons, Ignatius and John Barton, were evidently of age, and most likely married. The latter soon moved to Kentucky. His mother and at least one of her single daughters, *Rebecca,* accompanied him. The Cartwright's Creek Catholic Settlement was mainly composed of emigrants from Charles County. So there they also procured homes among their friends, relations, and acquaintances.

However, *Rebecca Montgomery* could not have been long in her new abode before she became the wife of *William Cambron,* one of *John Baptist's* sons. They were married in December, 1792, by Father William Rohan (or, as some say, De Rohan). The record is in both Bardstown and Springfield — possibly because Washington County was cut out of Nelson just at that time.[6] Tradition, as stated in the first paper, tells us that their homestead was that whereon the writer himself was born.

CAMBRON LIST I

Baptist (John Baptist) Cambron and his wife *Nancy* (?).

THEIR CHILDREN:—

Henry—married Margaret Harbin.
Horace—married Eliza Beaven.
William—married *Rebecca Montgomery.*
John Basil—married Lucy Smith.

---

[6] Benedict Cambron, mentioned in the foreword, was not certain whether *William Cambron* married a Rebecca Riney or a Rebecca Montgomery. But the records at Bardstown and Springfield combine with our family tradition to place the matter beyond all question.

Thomas—married Jane Queen.
Joseph—married "Patricia" (Martha) Osbourn.
Stephen—married Mary Linthicum.
Monica—married William Osbourn. No issue.
Nancy Catherine—married Charles Blandford.
Laura—spinster.

CAMBRON LIST II

William and *Rebecca (Montgomery) Cambron.*
THEIR CHILDREN:—
Elizabeth—married Joseph Carrico.
Benedict—married Sally (or Sarah) O'Daniel.
Nancy—married *Joseph O'Daniel,* Jr.
Mary—married James O'Daniel.
Rose Anna—married James Raymond Herbert.
Hilary—married Caroline Osbourn.
Eliza—married (1st) Pius Osbourn, and (2ndly) Thomas Carrico.
Thomas Wilson—died young and single.

From *Nancy Cambron* and *Joseph O'Daniel,* Jr., the Cambron line of descent, as far as the writer's purpose is concerned, is identical with that given in the O'Daniel lists at the end of the preceding paper. It is unnecessary to repeat it here. We did not have the time necessary to trace the Montgomery line, with any degree of certainty, beyond *John* and *Henrietta (Jenkins?) Montgomery,* the parents of the *Rebecca* who married *William Cambron,* as noted in Cambron List I. Thus the Montgomery line, in so far as we can give it, is the same as that on the Cambron side, with the exception of the first grade. However, we saw indications that it comes down from the William and Mary Montgomery who were witnesses, in 1693, to the will of John Wheeler of Charles County. Besides, we have always understood that there was a remote relationship between our family and the early Montgomerys of Washington County, Kentucky, all of whom came from Charles County, Maryland.

We remember Eliza (Cambron-Osbourn) Carrico and James and Mary (Cambron) O'Daniel of Cambron List II. The O'Daniels mentioned in this list, it will be recalled from O'Daniel List I, belonged to the same family. Two others of them, it will also be remembered, married grandchildren of *Baptist* (or *John Baptist) Cambron*. Walter O'Daniel, whom we likewise recollect, married Nancy of John Basil and Lucy (Smith) Cambron; whilst Mary O'Daniel became the wife of Raphael of Henry and Margaret (Harbin) Cambron. Nuptial unions between blood connections were quite common in the early Catholic missions of Kentucky, for nearly all of the faith there were related. Thus still another O'Daniel married a Cambron—William of James and Mary (Cambron) O'Daniel took unto wife Lucinda of John Basil and Lucy (Smith) Cambron. William O'Daniel was a great-grandson of *John Baptist Cambron,* and Lucinda Cambron a granddaughter of the staunch pioneer. Then the writer has a niece married to a great-grandson of Walter and Nancy (Cambron) O'Daniel. These two are great-great-great-grandchildren of the venerable *Baptist*.[7]

---

[7] See O'Daniel List V.

All those given in Cambron List I are buried at Saint Rose's, with the exceptions of *John Baptist* himself, Horace, Thomas, and their wives. The remains of those mentioned in Cambron List II repose in the same graveyard, except perhaps Sally, or Sarah, (O'Daniel) Cambron, the wife of Benedict. Any number of the later descendants of *Baptist* are also laid to rest there, while scores of them are to be found in Catholic cemeteries through various parts of Kentucky, especially in the counties of Washington, Marion, and Nelson. Wherever they went, seldom has one of them forsaken the faith inherited from their Kentucky pioneer forefather; and such lapses, whenever they did happen, resulted from mixed marriages. *William* and *Rebecca (Montgomery) Cambron,* the writer's paternal great-grandparents, appear to have died close together in 1837. Laura Cambron, *Baptist's* spinster daughter, outlived all her brothers and sisters. Saint Rose's records tell us that on August 7, 1847, was buried "old Miss Laura Cambron, aged eighty-two years." This shows that she was born in 1765. Evidently she was among *John Baptist's* elder children. Often have we heard her spoken of in terms of high praise. She spent her last years with our paternal great-grandparents and grandparents. Our father was in his seventeenth year at the time of her death.

Doubtless Cambron List I does not give the issue of *Baptist* in the precise order of their births. At this distance of time, without the aid of documents, such a chronological arrangement would be impossible. In his will the aged pioneer, who had most likely already distributed by far the major part of his property, does not mention any of his children by name; and there is no other authoritative record to which one can have recourse. Henry is placed first because he is said to have been the eldest child, which seems to be borne out by the fact that he took the Oath of Fidelity in Charles County, Maryland. Horace is named next, for we discovered no record of his marriage in Kentucky, and therefore fancy he had married before going west. The other sons are arranged in accordance to the dates of their marriages. Although the three daughters come last in the list, they were hardly the youngest of the family. Laura was certainly among the eldest ones; and the fact that we found no trace of their weddings at either Bardstown or Springfield suggests that Monica and Nancy Catherine were matrons when they went to Kentucky.

In Cambron List II we followed the order which seemed to be indicated by *William Cambron's* will and the dates of his children's marriages. Thomas Wilson Cambron, named after the great English Dominican mentioned in the preceding paper, died before his father, and consequently is not noted in the will. Tradition, however, says he was the youngest of *William's* family, and that he died single.

Attention has been called to the many Cambrons in Kentucky. An idea of the number formerly in old Saint Rose's parish may be gleaned from the church records. From July 17, 1830, to August 15, 1848, the name appears on the baptismal registers, either as parent or sponsor, no less than sixty-three times. The parish has been since much narrowed in extent, and few, if any, of the patronymic live within its present boundary.

Yet *John Baptist Cambron's* descendants form a goodly part of the model congregation. The Montgomerys, or their descendants, are also still there in fair numbers. Both lines have been, and are now, well represented in our various Catholic sisterhoods. Strange to say, in spite of their loyalty to the faith, it would seem that the country has never had a priest by the name of Cambron. Indeed, the only two of the venerable *John Baptist Cambron's* descendants to enter the priesthood, as far as we know, are the Fathers O'Daniel and Somes mentioned at the close of the preceding paper. Edward (Brother Damian) Blandford, a great-great-grandson whose mother was a Cambron, is a member of the Xaverian Brothers. Some Montgomerys, but only a few, have belonged to the ranks of our Catholic clergy.

THE HAMILTONS AND THE McATEES

Like the Cambrons, or Camerons, the Hamiltons were among Scotland's nobility, and go back to the early history of that country. The City of Hamilton on the Clyde, in Lanark County, was most likely named from them. They and the Douglas family of the same county intermarried to such an extent that the two escutcheons were eventually combined, making a common coat of arms which retained the distinctive emblems of both houses.[1] From Lanark the Hamiltons gradually spread through all Scotland, into England and Ireland, and the rest of the English-speaking world. During the awful penal days in the British Isles, as was the case with all the noble families, many of them gave up their religion under the pressure of tyranny. However, a number clung to their faith even in the face of death. We find the name not infrequently among the English Catholics who exiled themselves on the Continent for the sake of their consciences. The last Catholic metropolitan of Scotland before the country became Presbyterian was John Hamilton, archbishop of Saint Andrews. He was hanged in 1571 because of his Catholicity.

Although want of time prevented a thorough study of the Hamiltons in Maryland, advantage was taken of other researches to "keep an eye out" for them. They

---

[1] We have no taste for heraldry. The reader is therefore referred to Mrs. Maria L. Hamilton's (pages 10 and 11) *Hamilton Family of Charles County, Maryland* for the Hamilton and Douglas coats of arms. However, we do not agree with her statement that the Hamiltons are of English origin.

were certainly in the colony before 1659. According to the very common phonetic spelling of the past the name is written both Hambleton and Hamilton. Those on the Eastern Shore, who appear to have come first, generally have the former spelling. Yet the same person sometimes appears under the two forms. Those on the Western Shore are nearly always given as Hamilton, which is the orthography now in almost universal use. They were in Baltimore, Anne Arundel, Calvert, Prince George's, and Charles counties. Whilst they were most probably not Catholics, Andrew, William, and John Hambleton of Talbot County, on the Eastern Shore, were evidently men of the same honest, broadminded spirit as the founders of the colony. In 1689 they signed an appeal to the English sovereigns, begging them to suppress the rebellion which unscrupulous politicians and rampant bigots, under the leadership of one notorious John Goode, had raised against the lord proprietary. The purpose of the uprising, which largely succeeded, was to wrest the palatinate from the hands of Catholics, to disfranchise those of the old faith, and to make it unlawful for them to hold any civic office whatever. No uglier crime soils the fair pages of Maryland history.

Family tradition assures us that the early Hamiltons of Charles County were Catholics when they arrived, and that they came to the colony in search of a place where they could practise their religion in freedom and safety. The fidelity shown to the faith by their descendants not only there, but also in other parts of Maryland, in Kentucky, and elsewhere corroborates the tradition. It has been handed down to us that they came

THE HAMILTONS AND McATEES 51

directly from Scotland. Mrs. Mary L. Kelley *(op. cit., page 12)* says the first were *John* and *Elizabeth (Burdit) Hamilton,* who arrived in 1674. The same author further informs us that *Mrs. John Hamilton's* parents, *Thomas* and *Verlinda (Cotton) Burdit,* had been in Maryland since 1659, and that *Mrs. Burdit* was a daughter of *William* and *Anna (Graves) Cotton.* Be that as it may, *John Hamilton* and wife settled in the Port Tobacco district of Charles County.[2] He did not live long after his arrival in America. However, he left at least two children:—

Alexander, who married *Elizabeth (Shircliff) Green,* widow of Francis Green, and daughter of *William* and *Mildred (Thompson-Wheeler) Shircliff;* and John, who married Elizabeth Harrison.

The documents of the day show that the Hamiltons of Charles County were associated with its leading Catholics, as well as stood high in the esteem of the community. Among those with whom they came into intimate contact were several with distinctively Irish patronymics, such as Dilehay, Maloney, McAtee, and Payne. Although the given name Patrick was then at least often borne by Scotchmen, and was not infrequently found among the Hamiltons abroad, it is not at all improbable that these latter connections had their part in its being repeated so often among the Hamiltons of Charles County, Maryland. There were several Patrick Hamiltons in that part of the colony before

---

[2] Port Tobacco was formerly the capital of Charles County. Now, since the transfer of the seat of government to La Plata, the place scarcely deserves the name of a village. The first convent of nuns (Carmelites) in the United States was located at Port Tobacco.

the War of Independence. In any case, it is a sign of genuine Catholicity. Two at least of *Leonard Hamilton's* descendants in Kentucky still bear that baptismal name.

The Hamiltons in Charles County were loyal subjects of the colony. Several of them fought in the French and Indian War, which led to the loss of Canada by France to England by the Treaty of Paris, February 10, 1763. In like manner, when the American Revolution broke out, those who were of soldier age took the Oath of Fidelity to the patriot cause and bravely enlisted in the army.

Alexander and *Elizabeth (Shircliff-Green) Hamilton* had six children, who will be shown in Hamilton List II. Their fourth son (and fifth child) was named *Patrick*. He married *Ann* daughter of *Francis* and *Elizabeth (Wheeler) Green.*[3] This *Patrick Hamilton* had at least nine children, five sons and four daughters. Their names will be given in Hamilton List III. *Leonard Hamilton,* apparently *Patrick's* first son and certainly one of the eldest of his family, was an ensign in the Charles County militia during the American Revolution. He married *Nancy McAtee.* She belonged to Charles County, but we could not learn the names of her parents. This union was blessed with eleven children, of whom we shall tell in Hamilton List IV.

Although they had a large family and were well fixed in the Port Tobacco district, southern Maryland, *Leon-*

---

[3] Among the Catholics of early Maryland, as among those of Kentucky, there were all kinds of crisscross marriages in order to find life-partners within the fold of the Church.

ard and *Nancy (McAtee) Hamilton* joined in the western tide of emigration at the head of a band of homeseekers. This is said to have been in 1791. His name appears in the 1790 census of Charles County, which shows that he was there then, and suggests that he had not yet determined on going to Kentucky. The decision was doubtless in behalf of the temporal welfare of his children. Although the Cartwright's Creek Settlement was principally composed of people from Charles County, *Leonard Hamilton* located about where Lebanon now stands, or between that Catholic colony and the one on the Rolling Fork. His daughter Mary, married Benedict Spalding, Jr., (commonly called "Ben. Slick"), who initiated the town, and seems to have laid out a part of it on land obtained through his first wife, Mary Hamilton. In the boyhood days of the writer, a fountain almost within a stone's throw of the brick house in which this Benedict Spalding lived and died was still called the "Leonard Hamilton spring." Our oldest relations, many of whom knew *Leonard's* son *Clement* well, used to say that it supplied the pioneer settler's household with water.[4]

We have before us photostat copies, furnished by Mrs. Mary L. Kelley, of two letters of this *Leonard Hamilton* to his sister, Mrs. Elizabeth McAtee, who dwelt on Deer Creek, Harford County, Maryland. The first is dated November 24, 1795, and states that he lives on the Rolling Fork; but that no doubt was be-

---

[4] This Benedict J. Spalding was married three times, but had no children. The writer's mother was one of his many collateral heirs. A portion of his house still stands; and the yard extends to the western side of the Saint Rose-Lebanon Turnpike just where it leaves the road to Springfield.

cause his home was on the outskirts of the Catholic settlement named after that little river, which is not more than five miles from the present Lebanon. His wife, *"Nancy,"* never enjoyed such good health as she does in Kentucky. He is getting nicely settled in his new abode, and has also procured plantations for his two eldest sons, *Clement* and George. He would be glad if his sister, Mrs. McAtee, would come to the same neighborhood. Her children would not then be obliged to move far away from her, for they could readily obtain land in the vicinity. His greatest privation is that of regular religious services. He sends kindest regards to Father Boarman (either John or Silvester), one of the Jesuit missionaries with whom he had evidently been an intimate friend back in Maryland.

Here we may note that the farm which *Leonard Hamilton* bought for his son *Clement,* our great-grandfather, lies about half way between Lebanon and where we were born, and some two or two and a half miles from *Leonard's* own homestead. The Saint Rose-Lebanon Turnpike now runs by it. From *Clement* it passed to his youngest son, Leonard. We remember when this Leonard Hamilton sold it to one Clement Hill. It has been for some years in the possession of Wallace Parrott. We can not say where the plantation procured for George Hamilton lay. However, he did not live on it long, for in **1796** or **1797** he moved to Perry County, Missouri, with his father-in-law, Joseph Fenwick. Father Stephen Theodore Badin was the only priest in Kentucky at this time. Accordingly one of the reasons that induced Joseph Fenwick and George Hamilton to migrate to Missouri, which was then a

Spanish possession, was the hope of finding better facilities there for practising their religion.

Leonard Hamilton's second letter, dated April 10, 1815, begins with an apology for not visiting his sister, Mrs. McAtee, in Harford County (eighty or ninety miles from his old home, Charles County), while he was in Maryland from April to November, 1813. The illness and death of his sister Mary, the difficulties of the war times, and other affairs held him in Charles County so long that he was obliged to hurry back to Kentucky. He is glad that peace has been concluded on honorable terms, though the martial spirit runs high in his part of the country. One of his sons-in-law, whom he does not name, was killed in the Battle of New Orleans.[5]

The two documents reveal a kindly character and a strong family affection. Indeed, tradition still pictures the early settler as a man with these traits. Accustomed to the milder discipline of the Jesuit missionaries in Maryland, *Leonard Hamilton* and *Benedict Spalding,* Sr., like many of the other pioneers, did not take kindly to the stern and more or less Jansenistic regulations of Fathers Stephen Theodore Badin and Charles Nerinckx. Yet we recall a letter of Father Badin to Archbishop John Carroll, in which he says *Hamilton* and *Spalding* are the two leading men of the Rolling Fork Settlement. The number of their descendants

---

[5] This son-in-law was certainly one of the following four—a Mr. Luckett, a Mr. Bland, William James, or Ignatius Hagan. It will be recalled that the battle at New Orleans was the last in our war with England in 1812-1814. It took place on January 8, 1814, two weeks after the treaty of peace had been signed at Paris, December 24, 1813, but before word was received of the conclusion of hostilities. There were then no cables or telegraphs to carry the news quickly.

who have become priests and entered our various sisterhoods is evidence of their profoundly religious spirit. Hamilton's first letter seems to imply that he took two of his sisters (Anna and Henrietta) and their families to Kentucky with him. Mrs. Kelley (*op. cit.*, page 19) also says they went there. But we do not know whom they married, or just where they settled.

Other relations of the sturdy pioneer went from Maryland to Kentucky about the same time. In a letter of April, 1796, Father Badin tells Archbishop Carroll that the missive is to be carried to him by William Hamilton. This man was probably a brother of *Leonard;* but he does not seem to have lived in the Rolling Fork Settlement, or in that on Cartwright's Creek. The same document informs the archbishop that a George Hamilton has purchased a large tract of land on the Green River, and is anxious to start a Catholic colony there. We are inclined to think that this gentleman was a son of Samuel Hamilton, another brother of *Leonard* who Mrs. Kelley says emigrated to the Land of Blue Grass. Evidently he was not *Leonard's* son George.

Thomas and Ann (Hodgkins) Hamilton settled with their family near the present village of Fredericktown, Washington County, Kentucky, in 1797 or 1798. A strong, persistent tradition among the descendants of both Thomas and *Leonard* represents them as brothers. However, Mrs. Kelley (*op. cit.*, pages 14, 18, and 33) says Thomas was a son of James Hamilton. In that case, Thomas and *Leonard* were first cousins, not brothers, for *Leonard's* father was Patrick Hamilton, a brother of James. Be the relationship what it may, many of Thomas Hamilton's posterity still live in Washington County, and are people of the highest respectability as well as of staunch Catholicity.[6]

Leonard and *Nancy (McAtee) Hamilton's* large family were very likely all born in Maryland—in the Port Tobacco district. It is possible that two of their daughters, Elizabeth and Ann, were married before they left Charles County, for we could find no records of their marriage licenses at either Bardstown or Springfield, Kentucky. *Clement* was not long in the new west when he took unto wife *Nancy,* daughter of *Benedict J.* (Senior) and *Alethea (Abell) Spalding* of the Rolling Fork Settlement. *Clement* and *Nancy (Spalding) Hamilton* were joined in wedlock by Father William Rohan (or, as some call him, De Rohan), August 7, 1792. Both of them lived to extreme old ages. Their first children seem to have died in infancy or early youth. But seven of them, four sons and three daughters, became fathers and mothers of large familes.

Clement's third son, and the fifth of the issue who attained maturity, was *William Thompson Hamilton.* As shown in the paper on the O'Daniels, he married *Lucy,*

---

[6] *Patrick Hamilton* (List III) did not mention all his children in his will. But by dint of untiring perseverance Mrs. Maria L. Kelley discovered the rest in various other documents. Nowhere could she find a Thomas among them. From this fact she concluded that the Thomas Hamilton who married Ann Hodgkins and went to Kentucky was a son of James, who certainly had a child of that first name. However, the writer often heard his maternal grandmother, who married a grandson of *Leonard,* and Father Walter Hill, S.J., who was a grandson of Thomas, say that the two men were brothers. Mr. Webb *(op. cit.,* page 73) tells us the same story. Thomas Simms and Benedict Cambron (both mentioned in the foreword), as well as other old people, also frequently told us that the two early Kentucky Hamiltons *(Leonard* and Thomas) were brothers german.

the youngest child of *George* and *Sarah Ann (Edelen) Edelen,* who lived on Cartwright's Creek at the southeastern corner of "the Hamilton neighborhood" mentioned in the foreword and elsewhere. This was in late August or early September, 1826, for the marriage license is dated August 26 of that year. Their homes were not far apart. Prior to the erection of a Catholic church in Lebanon (1815), their parents were possibly the most southerly families in Saint Rose's parish. *William T. Hamilton* was exactly one year younger than his wife. The fourth child, but second daughter, of *William T.* and *Lucy (Edelen) Hamilton, Sarah Ann* (always called *Nancy),* became the second wife of *Richard Jefferson O'Daniel,* whose first name was popularly abbreviated to *Jeff.* No doubt the reader will recall this last couple from the story of the O'Daniels. A later paper will tell of the Edelens. Suffice it here to say that *William T. Hamilton* was one of the leading men of Marion County, which was taken from that of Washington eight or nine years after he married *Lucy Edelen.*

As the name indicates, the McAtees hailed from Ireland. They were Catholics. Doubtless, like many others of their faith, they came to Maryland in search of a refuge from the cruel religious persecution which then prevailed in the Emerald Isle. Charles County seems to have been their first American home. They stood high in the colony. The earliest mention of the patronymic the writer discovered was late in the seventeenth century. In a will of Ann, widow of James Browne, probated February 5, 1698, Patrick McAtee is shown as executor and sole legatee. Very likely he was her brother. How long he had been in Charles County we can not say. His wife's first name was Rosamond. Both of them appear to have died in 1717. Anthony Neale is not only a witness to Patrick McAtee's will, probated March 16, 1717, but is also appointed adviser to his wife. Here again we have a splendid Catholic association. Her will, possibly by some clerical error, bears the same date as that of her husband.

From the two foregoing wills we learn that to Patrick McAtee and his wife Rosamond were born Edmond, Patrick, James, Catherine, Mary, Eleanor, and Rosamond. Patrick married Sarah, daughter of Robert Greene, a grandson of the Thomas Greene, who came over with the Ark and the Dove, was a staunch Catholic, and had been a colonial councillor and once acting governor of Maryland. Catherine married a man by the name of Gallagher; Mary espoused a Mr. Boswell; whilst Eleanor and Rosamond became the wives of two gentlemen with the patronymic of Clements—probably brothers. *The Maryland Calendar of Wills* does not yet come down far enough for a further study of the McAtees, whilst it is morally, if not even physically, impossible for the writer to continue his researches through the records of Charles and other counties. However, the intimate connections between the McAtees and the Hamiltons, together with the fact that Patrick was a somewhat favorite given name among the latter in Kentucky, makes it quite probable that the *Nancy McAtee* who married *Leonard Hamilton* was a lineal descendant (a granddaughter, or great-granddaughter) of the first Patrick McAtee.

The extant military records of Maryland for the day

show that a number of the McAtees bore arms in our cause during the American Revolution. Several of them emigrated to Kentucky about the same time as *Leonard Hamilton,* if they did not even accompany him thither. Some of these latter located in the Rolling Fork Settlement, on the edge of which he himself settled.

HAMILTON LIST I

John and *Elizabeth (Burdit) Hamilton.*
THEIR CHILDREN:—
Alexander—married *Elizabeth (Shircliff) Green.*
John—married Elizabeth Harrison.

HAMILTON LIST II

Alexander and *Elizabeth (Shircliff-Green) Hamilton.*
THEIR CHILDREN:—
John—married Sarah Stewart.
William—died single.
James—married Mary Ann Coombs.
Mary—married John Stewart.
Patrick—married *Ann Greene.*
Samuel—married Elizabeth Greene.

HAMILTON LIST III

Patrick and *Ann (Greene) Hamilton.*
THEIR CHILDREN:—
Leonard—married *Nancy McAtee.*
William—married Violetta Hagan.

THE HAMILTONS AND McATEES

Elizabeth—married George McAtee.
Samuel—married Mrs. Christina (Smith) Clements.
Edward—married (1st) Mary Ann Boarman; (2ndly) Eleanor Hawkins.
Mary—died single.
Henrietta.
Anna.
Patrick—married and left a son Francis Patrick.[7]

HAMILTON LIST IV

Leonard (died in 1819) and *Nancy (McAtee) Hamilton*.[8]

THEIR CHILDREN:—

Elizabeth—married a Mr. Luckett.
Ann—married a Mr. Bland.
Clement—married *Nancy* of *Benedict J.* (Sr.) and *Alethea (Abell) Spalding*.
George Alexander—married Clara of Joseph Fenwick and wife.
Martha—married William James.
Anastasia—married Ignatius Hagan.
Henrietta—married Richard of *Benedict, Sr., and Alethea (Abell) Spalding*.
Harriet—married (1st) Livingston Thurman; (2ndly) John Thomas.
Mary—married Benedict J. Spalding, Jr., of *Benedict, Sr., and Alethea (Abell) Spalding*.

---

[7] If the Thomas Hamilton mentioned in the previous note was a son of Patrick, there were ten children in the family—six sons and four daughters.

[8] Leonard's will was probated September 13, 1819. Evidently his wife died earlier.

Leonard—married Mary Ann Beaven.
Samuel—married Elizabeth Delia Thomas. No issue.

HAMILTON LIST V

Clement—born in 1771 and died in 1859; and *Nancy*—born February 8, 1771, and died in 1863—*(Spalding) Hamilton.*

THEIR CHILDREN:—

Benedict Patrick—married (1st) Theresa Jarboe; (2ndly) Elizabeth ———.
Edward—married Alethea of *George* and *Sarah Ann (Edelen) Edelen.*
Elizabeth—married Benedict of *George* and *Sarah Ann (Edelen) Edelen.*
Anastasia—married Raymond Shircliff.
William Thompson—married *Lucy* of *George* and *Sarah Ann (Edelen) Edelen.*
Allie—died single and in young womanhood.
Leonard — married "Peggy" (Margaret) of George and Mary (Maddox) Carrico.

HAMILTON LIST VI

William Thompson—born June 6, 1806, and died June 22, 1856; and
Lucy (Edelen) Hamilton. She was born June 6, 1805, and died January 29, 1895.

THEIR CHILDREN:—

1. Benedict—married Mary Ellen of Benedict and Mary Ann (Lanham) Wheatley.

2. Clement — married Sally of Benedict and Sarah (Haydon) Downs.
3. Priscilla—married (1st) Charles of Andrew M. and Elizabeth (Russell) Mudd; (2ndly) Edward of "Nace" (Francis Ignatius) and Theresa (Carrico) O'Bryan.
4. *Sarah Ann* (or *Nancy*)—married *Richard Jefferson* of *Joseph* and *Nancy (Cambron) O'Daniel.*
5. Margaret—married James of Andrew M. and Elizabeth (Russell) Mudd.
6. Martin—married Victoria of Joseph and Mary Catherine (Medley) Osbourn.
7. Leonard—married (1st) Sarah of Joseph and Margaret Catherine (Mudd) Russell—no issue; (2ndly) Catherine of Henry and Cordelia (Nichols) Hagan.
8. William—died young and single.
9. "Zabe" (Eusebia)—married Robert of "Leck" (Alexander) and Sarah (Hagan-Boone) Craycroft.
11. Robert—married Mary Jane, widow of William M. Spalding, and daughter of James and Martina (Wheatley) O'Daniel.
12. Magdalen—married Edward C. of Joseph and Mary Dillama (Hoskins) Blandford.

HAMILTON LIST VII

Henrietta of *Leonard* and *Nancy (McAtee) Hamilton* and Richard of *Benedict* and *Alethea (Abell) Spalding.*

THEIR CHILDREN:—

Richard—married Mary Jane Lancaster.
Leonard—married (1st) Catherine Lancaster, (2ndly) Elizabeth Shadburn.
The Most Rev. Archbishop Martin John Spalding.
The Very Rev. Benedict J. Spalding, D.D.
Clement—died single.
Constantia—first wife of Hoskins Hamilton of Thomas and Ann (Hodgkins) Hamilton.
Julia—Sister Perpetua, a Lorettine Nun.[9]

In the first three family lists of this paper we followed the exquisite little book of Mrs. Maria L. (Hamilton) Kelley, who gave years of study and research to the Hamiltons of Charles County, Maryland, from whom she is descended.[10] With two exceptions we were guided in the arrangement of *Leonard* and *Nancy (McAtee) Hamilton's* children (List IV) by the dates of their marriages. The fact that we discovered no records in Kentucky of the marriage licenses of Elizabeth and Ann (respectively Mrs. Luckett and Mrs. Bland) indicates that they were married before they left Maryland, and that they were very likely the eldest of the family. Accordingly we placed them at the head of the list. Both of them are mentioned in *Leonard's* will, but without the first names of their husbands.

---

[9] Under the circumstances it is impossible to make out a genealogical line of the McAtees.

[10] Nevertheless, wherever possible, we checked up Mrs. Kelley's statements with our own notes. She was certainly careful and thorough in her work. There are a number of other Hamiltons in the Washington County census of 1810. However, as they evidently did not belong to our direct lines, we made no effort to trace them.

Leonard Hamilton, as shown by the Springfield records, signed the marriage bonds of his other five daughters in his own hand.[11] Neither Henrietta nor Mary (respectively Mrs. Richard and Mrs. Benedict Spalding) appear in their father's last will and testament. Both died before the document was drawn up. Mary left no issue; whilst Henrietta's children were doubtless passed over either because they had already received their portion, or because their father was wealthy in his own name. To our personal knowledge the descendants of Richard and Henrietta (Hamilton) Spalding to this day glory in having the venerable pioneer *Leonard* as one of their ancestors.

The order in which the children of *Clement* and *Nancy (Spalding) Hamilton* are placed (List V) is that given us by both the Benedict Cambron mentioned in the foreword and Mrs. Rose (Hamilton) Mackin, the latter of whom is their granddaughter. Hamilton List VI shows the issue of *William T.* and *Lucy (Edelen) Hamilton,* the writer's mother, uncles, and aunts. List VII properly belongs to the paper on the Spaldings. However, we have placed it in that on the Hamiltons in order to give the reader a better idea of the spiritual vocations among the descendants of *Leonard* and *Nancy (McAtee) Hamilton.* Some of these divine callings are often mentioned as a tribute to *Benedict* (Sr.) and *Alethea (Abell) Spalding.* They are no less to the honor of *Leonard* and *Nancy (Mc-*

---

[11] A comparison of these signatures with the handwriting in the photostat copies of *Leonard Hamilton's* two letters to his sister, Mrs. Elizabeth McAtee, proved the identity of their writer beyond any doubt.

Atee) Hamilton, to whose line of descent they equally belong.

Through their daughter Henrietta (List IV), who married Richard Spalding, *Leonard* and *Nancy (McAtee) Hamilton* were the grandparents of the Most Rev. Martin John Spalding, bishop of Louisville, archbishop of Baltimore, a writer, scholar, and orator of note, and one of the great prelates of the country; the Very Rev. Benedict J. Spalding, D.D., vicar general of the Diocese of Louisville; and Sister Perpetua, a saintly Lorretine Nun. Through Richard M. Spalding (of the Richard mentioned above), who married Mary Jane Lancaster, they were the great-grandparents of the late Most Rev. John Lancaster Spalding, bishop of Peoria, titular archbishop, and not less capable and distinguished in every way than his revered uncle, Martin John Spalding; of another Rev. Benedict J. Spalding, an exemplary and beloved priest who labored for a while in Kentucky, but died in the Diocese of Peoria; of Richard Spalding, who was drowned almost on the eve of his priestly ordination; and of the late Madam Henrietta Spalding, a noted member of the Ladies of the Sacred Heart in Saint Louis. Again, through Leonard Hamilton Spalding, a brother of the four last persons named who married Mary Heffernan of Louisville, the same pioneer Hamilton couple were the great-great-grandparents of the Rev. Martin John Spalding, now the admired pastor of Chillicothe, Illinois.

Two of the sons of *Leonard* and *Nancy (McAtee) Hamilton* were the fathers of very distinguished priests in their day. George A. Hamilton (List

THE HAMILTONS AND McATEES 67

IV), who married Clara Fenwick, went to Perry County, Missouri, where all their children, except the eldest, were born. Their son, named after his father, was one of the first two students whom Bishop Joseph Rosati of Saint Louis sent to Rome. There he was ordained on Christmas eve, 1837, returning to America in the fall of 1838. The early years of the priesthood of this Father George A. Hamilton were spent in a part of Illinois then under Bishop Rosati's jurisdiction and in the City of Saint Louis itself. In 1847 he became affiliated with the Diocese of Boston, and labored for a while on the missions of Vermont, but was soon appointed pastor of Saint Mary's, Charlestown, which is a part of the City of Boston. He built several churches, and made many converts wherever he toiled. In Boston he belonged to the bishop's council, as well as played a conspicuous part in diocesan affairs. He died in Charlestown July 31, 1874. His death caused a profound and wide-spread regret. He had two sisters, Matilda and Eulalia, who were outstanding characters among the Ladies of the Sacred Heart in Saint Louis during the early years of the community. They were therefore granddaughters of *Leonard* and *Nancy (McAtee) Hamilton.*

Another Rev. George A. Hamilton, sometimes called George A., Jr., was the son of Leonard and Mary Ann (Beaven) Hamilton. This Leonard was one of the younger children of *Leonard* and *Nancy (McAtee) Hamilton* (List IV). Although born in the part of Washington County, Kentucky, later taken to form that of Marion, Father George A. Hamilton, Jr., seems certainly to have studied for the Diocese of Saint Louis.

No doubt he was drawn thither by his reverend namesake and first cousin, of whom we have just told. However, he afterwards offered himself to the new Diocese of Chicago, for which he was ordained by Bishop William Quarter August 19, 1846. From that time until 1856 or 1857 this fourth sacerdotal grandson of *Leonard* and *Nancy (McAtee) Hamilton* did yeoman's service on the missions of Illinois, erecting churches as well as making converts. He then went to teach at Saint Thomas' College, Sinsinawa, Wisconsin, conducted by the Dominican Fathers, whom he seems to have thought of joining. While there he translated, from the French, the Abbé Thomas' volume of short sermons for the Sundays and feast-days of the year. The work is well done, for Father Hamilton was a man of good parts as well as highly educated; and the book long stood the clergy throughout the United States in good part.

In 1858 Father George A. Hamilton, Jr., became affiliated with the Diocese of Fort Wayne, Indiana, which had just been established and was in great need of priests. Here also he did herculean work on the missions, as well as built a number of churches. His last charge was Saint Mary's, Lafayette. In May, 1874, he accompanied the Most Rev. Joseph Dwenger, bishop of Fort Wayne, on the first American pilgrimage to Rome. Less than a year later, April 8, 1875, the faithful priest died rather suddenly, "after a most successful pastorate of eleven years" at Lafayette, and was buried under Saint Mary's Church. The author of *The Diocese of Fort Wayne* (page 113) is in error when he says that Father George A. Hamilton, on his mother's side, was descended from the Spaldings of Kentucky. His Spalding relationship came from his father, whose sister Henrietta married Richard Spalding, and was an ancestor of the Spaldings to whom we have called attention. Father Hamilton inherited considerable means, all of which he left to charity.

Scores of the descendants of *Leonard* and *Nancy (McAtee) Hamilton* have become nuns in the communities of Loretto, Nazareth, and Saint Catherine's, in Kentucky. A number of them are still to be found in those institutions. Others have entered our sisterhoods in various places. Edward (Brother Damian) Blandford, the Xaverian Brother mentioned at the close of the paper on the Cambrons, and now at Saint Mary's Industrial School, Baltimore, is a great-great-great-grandson of *Leonard Hamilton* and his wife. We also know of four living priests descended from those two early Catholic settlers of Kentucky. The Rev. Martin John Spalding of Chillicothe, Illinois (already noticed), and the Very Rev. Victor F. O'Daniel, O.P., S.T.M., Litt.D., whose works have given him an international reputation as a scholar and writer, are their great-great-grandsons. Father Felix Johnson of the Diocese of Louisville and Father Sydney Cyril Osbourn, O.P., are great-great-great-grandsons. Father Johnson's mother was a Hamilton, whilst Father Osbourn's maternal grandmother bore the same patronymic. Joseph (Brother Matthew) Osbourn, another great-great-great-grandson, is a professed member of the Order of Saint Dominic, and nearing the time of his ordination.

Quite a number of the descendants of *Leonard* and *Nancy (McAtee) Hamilton* still live in Marion and Washington counties or other parts of Kentucky. Not a few are scattered here and there throughout the United States. Everywhere, in so far as we have been able to learn, they have held nobly to the religion of their staunch forebears who helped to plant the faith in the Land of Blue Grass.

Leonard and *Nancy (McAtee) Hamilton,* the parents of the persons mentioned in Hamilton List IV, were buried at Calvary, on the Rolling Fork. There also their son *Clement* and wife were laid to rest. At the same place or in Lebanon were buried Henrietta, Mary, Samuel, and very likely George, who is said to have died while on a visit to Kentucky from Missouri. It is of record that the remains of Harriet and her second husband, John Thomas, were laid to rest at Saint Rose's. George's wife no doubt was buried in Missouri, whilst Richard and Benedict J. Spalding, Jr., of whom Henrietta and Mary were respectively the first wives, found their final resting places in Lebanon. Where the others noted in that list repose we can not say.

Of the children of *Clement* and *Nancy (Spalding) Hamilton* (List V) Elizabeth and Anastasia, the latter of whom we remember, and their husbands, Allie, and Leonard and his wife, both of whom we also remember, are buried in Lebanon. Benedict Patrick, Edward, and *William T.* and their wives found their last resting places in the graveyard at Saint Charles'. *William's* wife, our maternal grandmother, did not die until we had almost completed our twenty-seventh year. The Hamiltons of List VI, the issue of *William Thompson* and *Lucy (Edelen) Hamilton,* are buried as follows—Benedict and wife in Harrison County, Missouri; Clement and wife in Lebanon; Priscilla and her two husbands, Margaret and Magdalen and their husbands, Leonard and his first wife, Robert and his wife at Saint Charles'; Zabe and her husband in Meade County, Kentucky; *Sarah Ann* (or *Nancy*) and her husband and Martin at Saint Rose's. Martin's wife and Leonard's second wife, the former the writer's godmother, and both ladies of venerable age, still live at this writing.

The lines of descent from *William T.* and *Lucy (Edelen) Hamilton,* in so far as the writer's purpose is concerned, are the same as those given in the third, fourth, fifth, and sixth lists of the paper on the O'Daniels. It is not necessary to repeat them here.

THE SPALDINGS, THE ABELLS, AND THE O'BRYANS

The honorable pedigree of the Spaldings goes back to at least the thirteenth century in England. Their headquarters were apparently the town of the same name in Lincolnshire, on the eastern shore of the island. Thence they spread throughout Great Britain. As was the case with all the noble English families, many of them fell away from the Catholic religion at the time of the so-called Reformation. Others of them clung to the faith of their forefathers with admirable fortitude. These latter were gradually reduced to poverty by the fines and confiscations imposed upon them because of their fidelity to the Mother Church. No doubt the desire to be able to serve God without molestation in accordance with the dictates of his conscience had its part in bringing the first of the patronymic to the Colony of Maryland, "the Land of Sanctuary." At least, so runs the family tradition; and we know that this was the motive which brought many of the early Catholic settlers to Lord Baltimore's palatinate.

Thomas Spalding of Saint Mary's County was the earliest of the name we discovered. He seems to have come over in 1657. The records of the day show him to have been a poor man at the time of his arrival; but he prospered in his new home. It was not long before he married *Catherine,* who lived with the family of one John Jarbeau, a patronymic later anglicized into Jarboe. John Jarbeau was one of the influential men of his day in Saint Mary's County. He hailed from Dijon,

THE SPALDINGS, ABELLS, AND O'BRYANS

France. *Catherine,* whose maiden name is lost to history, seems to have come to Saint Mary's County, Maryland, with him. She was very likely a niece of either Mr. or Mrs. John Jarbeau.[1]

Thomas and *Catherine Spalding* became the progenitors of the numerous Catholic Spaldings scattered through Maryland, Kentucky, and other places. *William,* who Mr. J. W. S. Clements thinks was their second son, married *Ann,* a daughter of *Thomas Jenkins,* a family name which still indicates social standing as well as the old faith and loyalty to the Church in the former Lord Baltimore Palatinate. *William Spalding* prospered even more than his father, becoming quite a wealthy man for that day. Some of his children married into the best families of the colony. His son *Benedict J.* married *Elizabeth Mattingly.* These two, says Mr. Clements, do not appear to have managed so well. However, they were the parents of another *Benedict J. Spalding* who throve splendidly both in Saint Mary's County, Maryland, and in his adopted State of Kentucky, where he left an honored name. This second *Benedict J. Spalding* married *Alethea Abell,* daughter of *Samuel* and *Eleanor (O'Bryan) Abell.*

An interesting story is told of the life of *Samuel* and *Eleanor (O'Bryan) Abell.* From the time of the Puritan rebellion against Lord Baltimore (Charles Calvert I) in 1689, under the iniquitous leadership of John Goode, until the American Revolution prejudice against the Church was so strong in Maryland that a

---

[1] Many Jarboes, the anglicized form of Jarbeau, still live in Maryland and Kentucky. In both states they are people of respectability and sterling faith.

Catholic could hold no civil office, or even exercise the right of franchise. Some of the less steadfast, though happily not very many, gave up their faith for earthly preferment. A few seem to have taken the despicable test oath with a mental reservation that they might escape the burden of the tyrannical laws. Another consequence of this sad state of things, for mixed marriages continued to a certain extent, was a not altogether infrequent pre-nuptial agreement (without Church sanction, of course) that the girls should be brought up in the religion of the mother, and the boys in that of the father. *Eleanor O'Bryan,* in the thoughtlessness of her youth, became a victim of such a contract. However, she later sought to make amends by prayer and good example.

The associations of the early Abells in Saint Mary's County, Maryland, leave no doubt about their Catholicity. Indeed, it is highly probable that, like many of their coreligionists, they came to the colony in the hope of being free from molestation in its practice. Their descendants are still nearly all Catholics there and in Kentucky, whither a number of the patronymic afterwards emigrated. Yet the *Samuel Abell* who married *Eleanor O'Bryan* and his father, whose name was also *Samuel,* were high sheriffs in Saint Mary's County and enjoyed other remunerative preferments. Furthermore, the records show them to have been associated with the Church of England, and acting as if they were members of it. However, there are clear indications that this was pure pretense—a matter of political expediency for their temporal advantage, all the while they remained Catholic at heart. Possibly the temptation was too great for them to overcome. At any rate, so the story goes, the *Samuel Abell* who married *Eleanor O'Bryan* passed as an Anglican. A prenuptial agreement was made that the sons should be brought up in his faith, while the daughters should be reared in that of the mother.

Nevertheless Mrs. Abel took care to instruct all the children, as well as to set them good example. When his son Philip had grown up to manhood, *Samuel Abell*, then high sheriff, took him to Leonardtown, the county-seat of Saint Mary's, in order to have him sworn in as his deputy. The ambitious father was stunned beyond measure by Philip's public refusal to take the anti-Catholic oath required of all office-holders. Nor anger, nor threats, nor persuasion could induce the sturdy young man to violate the Catholic conscience which he had inherited from his mother. *Samuel Abell* himself had the priest before his death, and died in open profession of the faith. No doubt the prayers of *Mrs. Eleanor (O'Bryan) Abell* played a part in this happy ending. For the reasons now to be seen, we may call this gentleman *Samuel Abell*, the third.[2]

Robert Abell of Saint Mary's County is the earliest of the family name we found in the colonial records, which style him Captain. He appears for the first time in the documents of 1649. Mr. Clements is very likely correct in his opinion that *Captain Robert Abell* was the father of *Samuel Abell*, the first, who certainly belongs to the writer's line of ancestry. This *Samuel Abell's* will was probated April 8, 1698. It shows that

---

[2] There are reasons for believing that *Samuel Abell*, the second, also quietly sent for the priest to prepare him for death.

he left two sons, John and *Samuel,* and his widow *Ann.* The wife's family name seems to have been *Gardiner.* *Samuel Abell,* the second, married a daughter of *Simon Hall,* whose first name appears to have been *Winifred.* They were the parents of *Samuel Abell,* the third, who married *Eleanor,* the brave daughter of *Philip O'Bryan* of whom we have told. High Sheriff *Samuel Abell,* the second, died about 1755; High Sheriff *Samuel Abell,* the third, in 1777. The latter's daughter *Alethea* became the wife of the *Benedict J. Spalding* who moved to Kentucky. It is worthy of note that the wills on which the names of the two Samuel Abells of high-sheriff ambition appear leave little or no doubt about their Catholic connections or their real faith. Robert and Samuel have been favorite first names among the Abells of both Maryland and Kentucky—another no uncertain index to the line of descent.

The O'Bryans and Bryans, with various phonetic spellings, go back in the records to the early years of Maryland. Bryan is the same name as O'Bryan with the "O" and the apostrophe omitted. Such omissions have been frequent in Irish patronymics. They were located in more than one part of the colony. Everywhere, even were the name itself not a proof of the fact, their associations would show that they hailed from Ireland. Doubtless many of the descendants of those on the Eastern Shore, because of the lack of priests, were lost to the faith. On the Western Shore they remained as true to Catholicity as their coreligionists in Saint Mary's and Charles counties, whose loyalty was of the truest. The court records show that they prospered, and were held in high esteem. Bryantown, Charles

County, gets its name from them. To this day the patronymics O'Bryan and Bryan in Kentucky, whither a number emigrated, denote that the bearers of them are Catholics and descendants from the early settlers of southern Maryland. Thus it is easy to see the error of those who have represented the grandmother of Archbishop Martin John Spalding as direct from Ireland, and write her name O'Brien. They were not familiar with the colonial records of southern Maryland, in which that spelling never occurs.

The first of the name we found on the Western Shore was John Bryan of Saint Mary's County, whose "child" is mentioned, together with "the Roman Catholic Church," in the will of John Thimbellby in 1659. Then comes *Mathias O'Bryan* in 1673, and Thomas O'Bryan in 1676—both in Charles County. However, Mr. J. W. S. Clements says that, by accidently discovering *Mathias O'Bryan's* name had been distorted into Bryant several times by the court clerk, he traced him back in the colony prior to 1640.[3] This *Mathias O'Bryan*, Mr. Clements thinks, had a son *Mathias*. The reason, a very logical one, is that the father of *Philip O'Bryan*, whose daughter married *Samuel Abell*, the third, was named *Mathias*, and the difference in the ages of this *Philip* and the first *Mathias O'Bryan* was too great for their relationship to have been that of son and father. Thus both *Philip's* sire and grandsire were named *Mathias*. These O'Bryans were well-to-do. The worldly ambition and wiliness of *Samuel Abell*, the

---

[3] There was a great deal of distorting of family names in the early records of Maryland and Kentucky.

third, make one suspect that he had an eye on *Eleanor O'Bryan's* estate when he sought her in marriage.

The Abells and O'Bryans, in proportion to their numbers, proved themselves patriotic in our cause during the American Revolution. But the Spaldings do not appear to have been very strongly in favor of breaking away from the mother-country. Possibly they placed little trust in the colonists who had shown themselves so anti-Catholic.

Benedict J. Spalding, the second, and his wife, the former *Alethea Abell,* were well fixed in Saint Mary's County, Maryland. Yet they determined to seek a home in the new west, of whose marvellous fertility they had heard so much. In **1790** or **1791**, therefore, they went to Kentucky with their nine or ten children. They settled in the valley of the Rolling Fork, near the present hamlet of Calvary, and about five miles from where Lebanon now stands. In fact, it is said that *Benedict J. Spalding* led a band of Catholic pioneers from Saint Mary's and Charles counties to Kentucky. However, the greater number of those in the Rolling Fork Settlement seem to have been from Saint Mary's County, where were the firesides of the Spaldings. He prospered in his new abode, and two or three more children were born to him there, swelling the number to twelve — six boys and six girls, all of whom will be shown in Spalding List IV. His house stood within a half-mile of the present Calvary, but on the opposite side of the little river. That part of the plantation is now owned by Robert Spalding.

As stated in the preceding paper, in Kentucky, *Nancy,* daughter of *Benedict J.* and *Alethea (Abell)*

Spalding, married *Clement,* son of *Leonard* and *Nancy (McAtee) Hamilton.* The Court records at Bardstown show that the ceremony took place August 7, 1792, and that the officiating clergyman was Father William Rohan, or De Rohan. There were two other marriages, it will be recalled, between the families of *Benedict J. Spalding* and *Leonard Hamilton,* by which Henrietta and Mary Hamilton became the first wives respectively of Richard and Benedict J. Spalding, Jr. *William Thompson Hamilton,* son of the *Clement* given above, married *Lucy,* daughter of *George* and *Sarah Ann (Edelen) Edelen* in late August or early September, 1826. *William T. Hamilton's* daughter *Sarah Ann,* always called *Nancy,* became the second wife of *Richard Jefferson,* or *"Jeff,"* *O'Daniel.* This ceremony took place in Saint Charles' Church, Marion County, February 14, 1860. Father Francis De Muelder officiated at it.[4] The children of this last couple are given in O'Daniel List III. All these unions were happy. With the exception of that of Mary Hamilton, who left no issue, they were blessed with large families.

Because of the lack of documents and the want of sufficient time for research, the knowledge obtained on the O'Bryans is not clear, definite, or complete enough for

---

[4] At Bardstown, the book in which a list of the persons married in Nelson County has been made generally shows the clergyman or official who officiated at the ceremony. The matrimonial book for Washington County, at Springfield, does not give this information; and none of the extant church records in Washington and Marion counties, except in the last instance mentioned here, go back far enough for our purpose. Those of Saint Charles' Church, in the latter county, as we understand, have been lately destroyed by fire. The court-house at Lebanon was burned during the Civil War by Major-General John H. Morgan of guerilla fame, and nearly all the records destroyed.

the arrangement of their line in lists as is done in the case of the other families. We will therefore put it this way:—*Mathias O'Bryan,* the first; *Mathias O'Bryan,* the second; *Philip O'Bryan,* whose daughter *Eleanor* married *Samuel Abell,* the third. We could not learn who were the wives of the three O'Bryan men. It seems quite certain that, including *Eleanor,* there were four American generations of that patronymic in the writer's line of descent.

The beginning of the Abell line is somewhat conjectural, and the lists under that name can not be filled out completely, or with absolute certainty. However, the descent seems to run in this wise:—

ABELL LIST I
Robert Abell and *Wife.*
THEIR CHILDREN:—
Richard (?).
Samuel—married *Ann Gardiner.*
William (?).

ABELL LIST II
Samuel and *Ann (Gardiner) Abell.*
THEIR CHILDREN:—
John.
Samuel—married Winifred (?) *Hall.*
Possibly others.

ABELL LIST III
Samuel and *Winifred (Hall) Abell.*
THEIR CHILDREN:—
Samuel—married *Eleanor O'Bryan.*
Very likely others.

ABELL LIST IV

Samuel and *Eleanor (O'Bryan) Abell.*

THEIR CHILDREN:—

Philip—married Ann Dryden.
Samuel—married Susan Spalding.
John.
Robert—married Margaret Mills.
Alethea—married *Benedict J.* of *Benedict J.* and *Elizabeth (Mattingly) Spalding.*
Winifred—married a Mr. Morgan.
Dorothy—married a Mr. Wimsatt.
Mary—apparently died single.
Eleanor.

SPALDING LIST I

Thomas and *Catherine Spalding.*

THEIR CHILDREN:—

John—married (1st) a Miss Field; (2ndly) Priscilla Smith.
William—married *Ann Jenkins* of *Thomas.*
Thomas—married Honora Cole.
Jacob (?).

SPALDING LIST II

William and *Ann (Jenkins) Spalding.*

THEIR CHILDREN:—

Thomas—married Catherine Cooper.
William.
Henry—married Mary—
Benedict J.—married *Elizabeth Mattingly.*

John Baptist.
Jeanne (Jane)—married a Mr. Plowden.
Mary—married a Mr. Seale.
Ann—married William Joseph.

SPALDING LIST III

Benedict J. and *Elizabeth (Mattingly) Spalding.*
THEIR CHILDREN:—
Henry—married a Miss Elder.
Benedict J.—married *Alethea* of *Samuel* and *Eleanor (O'Bryan) Abell.*
Probably others.

SPALDING LIST IV

Benedict J. and *Alethea (Abell) Spalding.*
THEIR CHILDREN:—
Nancy (born February 8, 1771, and died in 1863)—married *Clement* of *Leonard* and *Nancy (McAtee) Hamilton,* who was born in 1771, and died in 1859.[5]
Mary—married (1st) Henry Wathen; (2ndly) Edward Spalding.
Eleanor—married Basil Riney.
Richard—married (1st) Henrietta of *Leonard* and *Nancy (McAtee) Hamilton;* (2ndly) Henrietta Thompson; (3rdly) Mary Adams.
Thomas—married Susan Abell.
Elizabeth—married John Wathen.

---

[5] The Hon. Benedict Webb (*op. cit.,* page 111, note), possibly by a typographical error, makes *Clement Hamilton* die in 1851. He died in his eighty-ninth year, and his wife in her ninety-third.

THE SPALDINGS, ABELLS, AND O'BRYANS 83

Benedict J.—married (1st) Mary of *Leonard* and *Nancy (McAtee) Hamilton;* (2ndly) Eliza Elder; (3rdly) Eliza McElroy. No issue by any marriage.
Joseph—married Elizabeth Moore.
Catherine—married Richard Forest.
Louis Ignatius—married Ann Pottinger.
Alethea—married Francis Simms.
William—married Elizabeth Thompson.

The O'Daniel descent from *Nancy Spalding,* who married *Clement* of *Leonard* and *Nancy (McAtee) Hamilton,* is shown in the Hamilton lists V and VI and the O'Daniel lists III, IV, V, VI.

In regard to the early Spaldings, Abells, and O'Bryans we were largely guided by Mr. J. W. S. Clements' carefully written book mentioned in the foreword. In this we felt quite justified for the reason that, whenever possible, we compared his data with our own notes, and generally found him correct. In other cases his arguments appeared perfectly logical. The order in which we have placed the children of the Kentucky Catholic pioneers, *Benedict J.* and *Alethea (Abell) Spalding* is somewhat different from that we have seen given by others. But ours is taken from a list of them evidently copied from an old family Bible.

The three Hamiltons married to the children of *Benedict J.* and *Alethea (Abell) Spalding,* as we know from family tradition, the Springfield records, and otherwise, were a son and two daughters of *Leonard* and *Nancy (McAtee) Hamilton* (Hamilton List IV). Many a talk about this matter did the writer have with the Thomas W. Simms mentioned in the foreword. He was a son of Francis and Alethea (Spalding) Simms, and consequently a nephew of these parties. As the Benedict J. Spalding who married Mary Hamilton, although thrice married, had no issue and lived to a patriarchal age, the writer's mother was one of his many collateral heirs at the time of his death.

For the reasons given there, some vocations to the priesthood among the descendants of *Benedict J. and Alethea (Abell) Spalding* have been noticed in Hamilton List VII and thence on to the end of the preceding paper. To the clergymen mentioned there must be added the late Rev. Samuel B. Spalding of the Archdiocese of Philadelphia. He was a son of Samuel and Elizabeth (Lancaster) Spalding, a grandson of Joseph and Elizabeth (Moore) Spalding (Spalding List IV), and a great-grandson of *Benedict J. and Alethea (Abell) Spalding.* Two young priests of the same good stock are now laboring in the Diocese of Louisville—the Revs. Joseph L. Spalding and Charles C. Boldrick. Father Victor F. O'Daniel, O.P., Father Felix Johnson, Father Sydney C. Osbourn, O.P., Brother Joseph M. Osbourn, O.P., and Brother Damian Blandford, C.F.X., with all of whom the reader has become acquainted, are likewise descended from the two stalwart pioneer leaders of the Spaldings on the Rolling Fork. Perhaps none of the early Catholic families have been, or are now, better represented in our various sisterhoods scattered here and there than this noble couple.

Benedict J. and Alethea (Abell) Spalding were laid to rest in the graveyard at Calvary, near their home.

There also or in Lebanon were buried their many children and their consorts, with the exception of Eleanor and Alethea whose married lives were spent in the parish of Saint Rose, and Louis Ignatius, who settled in that of the Sacred Heart, Union County. Descendants of the two historic pioneers are today scattered almost throughout the United States. Fortunately, as a rule, they still remain true to the faith inherited from their ancestors in the early Catholic colony on the Rolling Fork, in what is now Marion County, Kentucky.

THE EDELENS

In the early documents of both Maryland and Kentucky the name Edelen, doubtless because of the sound, is sometimes written Edlen or Edlin, and not infrequently Edelin, by the court clerks. A few have retained this last spelling. But Edelen, we are sure, is the correct form; and it is the one now in almost universal use. It is an Anglo-Saxon word which means pure or noble. We have seen it asserted that the first of the patronymic in Maryland came over with the Ark and the Dove. However, there is no proof for such a statement. The earliest of the name we have found in the records was *Richard Edelen* (written this way), who was appointed executor of his estate by the will of Samuel Cressey of Saint Mary's County. The document is dated February 2, 1675, and was probated February 4, 1675. The same Edelen was also a witness to several wills of people in Saint Mary's County within the next few years. Evidently he was not a new-comer in that part of the colony.

Family tradition tells us that the pioneer was brought to "the Land of Sanctuary" by the hope of finding there a safe asylum for the practice of his religion. Doubtless this is true, for he ever stood out as a staunch Catholic. He was universally held in high esteem; and he prospered from the start. In 1693 the Puritan element in the adjoining county, Calvert, sent a petition to the colonial council urging that *Richard Edelen* should not be appointed public surveyor for Saint Mary's County on the ground that he was "a known Papist." It is possible, though hardly probable, that the victim of this display of religious intolerance was not the original pioneer himself, but a son with the same first name. From that time until the outbreak of the American Revolution, which put an end to the anti-Catholic laws of the colony, the name Edelen does not appear in the *Maryland Archives*. We need no better proof of the perseverance of the various branches of the family in the faith of their forefathers.

Richard Edelen, Sr., died the year after the outrageous protest against his holding a public office. His will (dated March 5, 1694, and probated July 31, 1694) leaves "Saint Christopher's," certainly in Saint Mary's County, to his son *Richard* and heirs. Sons Edward and Christopher and their heirs are given an estate in Charles County, which was called "Dublin." Son Thomas is bequeathed a tract of land "surveyed by William Humphery." Daughter Catherine is left personalty. But the home plantation in Saint Mary's County is to be equally divided among the five children. No doubt this will marks the beginning of the Edelens in Charles County, where a number of them are soon found. The land "surveyed by William Humphrey," which fell to Thomas, possibly lay in Prince George's County, for within a few years the patronymic, together with the given name of Thomas, had become common in that part of the colony. In Prince George's County there were intermarriages between the Edelens and the Queens and other well-known families which are a proof of both Catholicity and social prominence.

Similarly, the records of Charles County leave no doubt concerning the faith and character of the Edelens there. One of them married Elizabeth, daughter of Thomas Jenkins. Another became the wife of Basil Spalding. Still another married Sarah, daughter of Thomas Hagan. Richard Edelen was executor of the estate of John Smith, who died in 1705. Indeed, the names of those who are mentioned in the wills of that county in connection with Edelens show a galaxy of Catholics of whom any member of the faith might justly be proud. There is no tradition or evidence of any of them giving up their religion.

Others of the patronymic remained in Saint Mary's County for some years. These were at least *Richard Edelen,* the second, who is mentioned in his father's will, and his descendants. But whether the two Richards to whom we now call attention were the second and third, or the third and fourth, of that given name we can not say with certainty. The long intervening time makes the latter supposition the more probable. However it was, the will of *"Richard Edelen, Jr.,"* of Saint Mary's County, probated August 15, 1738, appoints his wife Margaret and his brother Philip executors of his estate. His father, *"Richard Edelen, Sr."* is named trustee of the property, "to rectify any mismanagement, for the good of the children."

As Saint Mary's County, which was emphatically Catholic and the first part of the colony to be settled, gradually filled up, many moved northward to Charles and Prince George's counties, where there were not a few of their coreligionists. In this way, practically all the Edelens seem to have left Saint Mary's County by the time of the American Revolution. *The Maryland Calendar of Wills* has so far been brought down only to the end of 1738, whilst lack of leisure and a crippled condition have prevented the writer from making an exhaustive study of the county records. Thus he has not been able satisfactorily to trace the Edelens of Charles County from that time to the War of Independence.[1] However, prior to that date (1738), we have several first or given names (in Saint Mary's and Charles counties) which continue among those of the patronymic in both Maryland and Kentucky—for instance, Richard, Edward, Thomas, Robert, and James. That of Richard has always been especially popular with them. This fact combines with a family tradition to prove that the pioneer of that given name, whom we first discovered in Saint Mary's County in 1675, was the original progenitor of the Maryland and Kentucky Edelens. He had evidently been in the colony for some time before that date, but just how long we can not say.

Liber X (10) in the Office of the Registry of Deeds, La Plata, Charles County, reveals ever so many Edelens who took the Oath of Fidelity to the American cause in the contest with England. One of those in the Newport Hundred, or district, in the southern part of the county, was called *George*. Others of the family took the same oath in Prince George's County. Besides, the *Archives of Maryland,* incomplete as they are, show several Edelens who fought on our side in the American Revolution.[2] These facts are proof positive of Edelen patriotism during that trying period.

---

[1] A good many of the records of Charles and Saint Mary's counties have been destroyed by fire or become corroded by time.

[2] The military records of Maryland for the American Revolution are admittedly quite incomplete.

Among the soldiers of the patronymic we find a number of given names which have since become of common use in Kentucky with the descendants of the original progenitor—Leonard, Henry, John, and *George*.

Family tradition convinces the writer that the last mentioned patriot, *George Edelen,* is one of his direct ancestors, or great-grandfathers. The same tradition has it that the soldier married a blood relation. Thus we have no doubt but that he was the *George Edelen* of Charles County, Maryland, who was joined in wedlock to *Sarah [Ann] Edelen* by Father Henry Pile in May, 1785.[3] Often did we hear our maternal grandmother, *Lucy (Edelen) Hamilton,* say that her mother's maiden name was *Sarah Ann Edelen;* that her father was *George Edelen;* that her parents were cousins; that they moved to Kentucky from southern Charles County; that her father had seen service in the War of Independence; and that our mother, though called *Nancy,* was named *Sarah Ann* after her grandmother.

The Catholic exodus from Maryland to Kentucky began the very year of the marriage of *George* and *Sarah Ann (Edelen) Edelen.* Soon several of the Edelens joined in the westward march. In 1795, or thereabouts, Joseph located in the Pottinger's Creek Settlement, whilst Samuel and the *George* of whom we have told secured homes in that on Cartwright's Creek. Tradition tells us that the two latter were closely related. *George,* the writer's great-grandfather, took his aged **father,** *Robert,* along with him. The land which he purchased lay at the southern end of the Cart-

---

[3] BRUMBAUGH, Gaius M., *Maryland Records: Colonial, Revolutionary, County, and Church,* II, 493.

THE EDELENS

wright's Settlement proper. His residence stood within a few hundred yards of where now stands (though somewhat changed) that in which the late Archbishop John Lancaster Spalding spent his youth. Richard M. Spalding, the archbishop's father, bought this Edelen estate. Until within twenty-five or thirty years ago a roof over a hole in the ground by the side of the Springfield-Lebanon Turnpike, which had served as an ice house, marked the place where *George Edelen* lived and died. Full many a time have we passed it. His name appears on a letter of appeal for a priest which the Catholics of the Cartwright's Creek Settlement sent Archbishop John Carroll of Baltimore sometime in 1803 or 1804. It is also given in the list of subscribers towards building Saint Rose's Priory, near Springfield, and the College of Saint Thomas of Aquin formerly connected with that institution.[4]

Mr. Webb *(op. cit.,* page **77**) confuses *George Edelen* with his father *(Robert)*, and expresses a belief that several of the younger man's children fell into the hands of non-Catholics after his death, and were not reared in the faith. Evidently the noted historian failed to get in touch with the proper persons for information about this really splendid Catholic family. Few of the early settlers of that colony had as many children as *George Edelen;* nor have the descendants of any of the Kentucky pioneers remained truer to their religion. There was one exception. *George's* son Leonard moved to Danville, Kentucky. There he grew careless, mar-

---

[4] For this letter to Archbishop Carroll and list of subscribers see O'DANIEL, Rev. Victor F., *A Light of the Church in Kentucky,* or *Life of the Very Rev. Samuel Thomas Wilson, O.P.,* pages 313-315 and 308-310.

ried a Presbyterian lady, and let her bring up the children in her own creed.⁵ The other ten children of *George* and *Sarah Ann (Edelen) Edelen* were certainly as representative of genuine Catholicity as those of Samuel Edelen, of whom Mr. Webb speaks in terms of high praise.

The eldest, if not even the greater number, of *George Edelen's* large family were born in Maryland. His house in Kentucky, which had disappeared prior to the writer's day of recollection, stood on the right side of Cartwright's Creek, and almost within a stone's throw of the stream. The list of subscribers for erecting Saint Rose's Priory and the College of Saint Thomas of Aquin (noted above), which belongs to from late 1806 to 1808, proves that he was living then. But the 1810 census of Washington County shows that he had died before it was taken, for his name does not appear therein. However, it gives his widow, *Sarah [Ann] Edelen,* with nine of her eleven children—three sons and six daughters. The Springfield records tell us that two had married—Alice in October, 1807, and Robert in February, 1808. Tradition also says they were settled in life before the death of their father.

It has been handed down to us that the remains of *Robert Edelen,* Sr., who no doubt was the first to die, and his son *George* were laid to rest in the little grave-

---

⁵ Leonard Edelen did not join his wife's church. Often did we hear our maternal grandmother, who was his youngest sister, tell how she went to see him during his last illness and entreated him to let her send for a priest. He declared that he had never given up his faith. However, he had lived so long without practising his religion that her exhortations were in vain. Two of his sons were afterwards merchants in Lebanon, and a cordial friendship existed between them and their Catholic relatives.

yard by the side of old Saint Ann's Church. Mrs. *Sarah Ann (Edelen) Edelen* was blessed with a long life. The records of Saint Rose's tell us that on July 20, 1848, was buried "old Mrs. *Sarah Ann Edelen,* aged eighty-five years." That places her birth in 1763. She spent her last years with her eldest son, Robert. Often did the writer hear his mother say that, although ever called *Nancy,* she was baptized with the name of *Sarah Ann* after her grandmother Edelen, whom she remembered well. As previously noted, his maternal grandmother, *Lucy (Edelen) Hamilton,* was also wont frequently to tell the same story. A search of the records of Saint Charles' Church, which we understand have been since destroyed by fire, proved their statements to be correct.

Lucy, the youngest of the eleven children of *George* and *Sarah Ann (Edelen) Edelen,* married *William Thompson Hamilton* of *Clement* and *Nancy (Spalding) Hamilton. Sarah Ann,* or *Nancy,* of *William T.* and *Lucy (Edelen) Hamilton* became the second wife of *Richard Jefferson,* or *"Jeff,"* of *Joseph* and *Nancy (Cambron) O'Daniel.* The descendants of *Richard J.* and *Sarah Ann (Hamilton) O'Daniel* are shown near the end of our first paper. It is quite certain that they are in direct line from the first *Richard Edelen.* It is almost certain that they are also in direct line from the second Edelen of that given name, if not even from the third and fourth. Yet, since (under the circumstances) we can not establish beyond all doubt the links between these earlier men and the *Robert* and *George Edelen* who went to Kentucky, the several Richards are omitted from the Edelen tables which follow.

EDELEN LIST I

Robert Edelen and *Wife*.

THEIR SON:—

George—married *Sarah Ann Edelen*.
Very likely other children.

EDELEN LIST II

George and *Sarah Ann (Edelen) Edelen*.

THEIR CHILDREN:—

Alice—married Thomas Medley.
Robert—married Hettie Riney.
Harriet—married Alexander of Thomas and Ann (Hodgkins) Hamilton. She was the first of Alexander Hamilton's four wives.
Priscilla—died a fairly aged spinster.
Elizabeth—married James Howard.
Alethea—married Edward of *Clement* and *Nancy (Spalding) Hamilton*.
Louise—married John Abraham Rhodes.
Benedict—married (1st) Elizabeth of *Clement* and *Nancy (Spalding) Hamilton;* (2ndly) Theresa Wright.
Leonard—married Susan Bruce.
James—married Rose of Joseph and Patricia Martha (Osbourn) Cambron.
Lucy—married *William Thompson Hamilton* of *Clement* and *Nancy (Spalding) Hamilton*.

For the descendants of this last couple, *William T.* and *Lucy (Edelen) Hamilton,* through their daughter *Sarah Ann*, who married *Richard Jefferson O'Daniel*, see O'Daniel lists III, IV, V, and VI. It is unnecessary to repeat them here. We could not learn the name of *Robert Edelen's* wife (Edelen List I), or whether he had more than one child.

George Edelen's large family (Edelen List II) are placed in the order suggested by the dates of their marriages and "Order Book C," not paginated, Office of the Register of Wills, Springfield, Kentucky.[6] Time and again did the writer hear *Lucy (Edelen) Hamilton,* his maternal grandmother (than whom no finer woman ever existed), say that she was the baby of the family, and that her father died when she was very small. The same tradition exists among all her living grandchildren, of whom there are still many. Besides her, we remember Benedict's second wife well. They both lived to extreme old ages. Benedict's first wife and *Lucy's* and Alethea's husbands, as may be seen from Hamilton List V and Edelen List II, were sister and brothers. *Lucy* and Alethea and their husbands are buried at Saint Charles'; Benedict and his two wives in Lebanon; Leonard, and most likely his wife, in Danville. All the others and their consorts, we think, repose in the graveyard at Saint Rose's. The descendants of the original pioneer *George Edelen* are now scattered through many parts of the United States. Everywhere, with the exception of those of his son Leonard, they have adhered to the Catholic faith with admirable fidelity. James and Rose (Cambron) Edelen at least are still represented in the parish of Saint Rose.

---

[6] The marriage licenses of all of them are in Springfield, except that of Leonard, who married in Danville.

SUMMARY OF DIRECT GENERATIONS

THE O'DANIELS:—

1. Joseph and Mary (O'Brien) O'Daniel.
2. Joseph, the second, and Nancy (Cambron) O'Daniel.
3. Richard Jefferson and Sarah Ann (Hamilton) O'Daniel.
4, 5, and 6. Their children, grandchildren, and great-grandchildren.

THE CAMBRONS:—

1. John Baptist, or Baptist, and Nancy Cambron.
2. William and Rebecca (Montgomery) Cambron.
3. Joseph and Nancy (Cambron) O'Daniel.
4. Richard Jefferson and Sarah Ann (Hamilton) O'Daniel.
5, 6, and 7. Their children, grandchildren, and great-grandchildren.

THE MONTGOMERYS:—

1. John and Henrietta (Jenkins?) Montgomery.
2. William and Rebecca (Montgomery) Cambron.
3. Joseph and Nancy (Cambron) O'Daniel.
4. Richard Jefferson and Sarah Ann (Hamilton) O'Daniel.
5, 6, and 7. Their children, grandchildren, and great-grandchildren.

THE HAMILTONS:—

1. John and Elizabeth (Burdit) Hamilton.
2. Alexander and Elizabeth (Shircliff-Greene) Hamilton.
3. Patrick and Ann (Greene) Hamilton.
4. Leonard and Nancy (McAtee) Hamilton.
5. Clement and Nancy (Spalding) Hamilton.
6. William Thompson and Lucy (Edelen) Hamilton.
7. Richard Jefferson and Sarah Ann (Hamilton) O'Daniel.
8, 9, and 10. Their children, grandchildren, and great-grandchildren.

THE O'BRYANS:—

1. Mathias O'Bryan, the first, and wife.
2. Mathias O'Bryan, the second, and wife.
3. Philip O'Bryan and wife.
4. Samuel and Eleanor (O'Bryan) Abell.
5. Benedict J. and Alethea (Abell) Spalding.
6. Clement and Nancy (Spalding) Hamilton.
7. William Thompson and Lucy (Edelen) Hamilton.
8. Richard Jefferson and Sarah Ann (Hamilton) O'Daniel.
9, 10, and 11. Their children, grandchildren, and great-grandchildren.

THE ABELLS:—

1. Robert Abell and wife.
2. Samuel, the first, and Ann (Gardiner) Abell.

98 O'DANIEL AND ALLIED ANCESTRY

3. Samuel, the second, and Winifred (Hall) Abell.
4. Samuel, the third, and Eleanor (O'Bryan) Abell.
5. Benedict J. and Alethea (Abell) Spalding.
6. Clement and Nancy (Spalding) Hamilton.
7. William Thompson and Lucy (Edelen) Hamilton.
8. Richard Jefferson and Sarah Ann (Hamilton) O'Daniel.
9, 10, and 11. Their children, grandchildren, and great-grandchildren.

THE SPALDINGS:—

1. Thomas and Catherine Spalding.
2. William and Ann (Jenkins) Spalding.
3. Benedict J., the first, and Elizabeth (Mattingly) Spalding.
4. Benedict J., the second, and Alethea (Abell) Spalding.
5. Clement and Nancy (Spalding) Hamilton.
6. William Thompson and Lucy (Edelen) Hamilton.
7. Richard Jefferson and Sarah Ann (Hamilton) O'Daniel.
8, 9, and 10. Their children, grandchildren, and great-grandchildren.

THE EDELENS:—

1. Robert Edelen and wife.
2. George and Sarah Ann (Edelen) Edelen.

DIRECT LINES

3. William Thompson and Lucy (Edelen) Hamilton.
4. Richard Jefferson and Sarah Ann (Hamilton) O'Daniel.
5, 6, and 7. Their children, grandchildren, and great-grandchildren.*

---

* The impossibility of tracing, with positive certainty, the lines of the O'Daniels, Cambrons, Montgomerys, and Edelens in Maryland, prior to those who went out to Kentucky, is the reason why fewer generations are given for those families. Otherwise the lines of the O'Daniels, the Montgomerys, and the Edelens would doubtless have been amongst the longest.

CONCLUSION

The earliest persons mentioned in these brief papers helped to plant the faith in Maryland, which is a cradle of Catholicity in the United States. They were real pilgrims for the sake of their consciences. With few exceptions, in spite of the persecution, hardships, and privations they were forced to undergo because of their religion, their descendants remained loyal and true to it. Maryland was perhaps the most élite of the original Anglo-American colonies. Its Catholics contributed not a little to make it such. It had no finer or more stalwart people than were they. We found no tories in the lines which we have endeavored to trace.

Those of the Maryland Catholics who went out to Kentucky, the first state admitted into the Union beyond the Alleghany Mountains, helped to plant the faith there and to make that commonwealth a cradle of Catholicity in the new west. In no part of the Land of Blue Grass did the Catholic religion take deeper or stronger root than in the settlements on Cartwright's Creek and the Rolling Fork, the localities in which practically all the pioneers noted in these pages made their homes and brought up their families. None contributed to this result more than they. Like their progenitors in Maryland, these same early Kentucky settlers were true-blue. Like their forefathers in the east again, they and their descendants have deserved well of both Church and State. Not a few of the latter have held high places in both Church and State with credit to themselves, no less than with benefit to their fellowman. As a rule, however, all down their respective lines these good people have been, and still are, of that sturdy agricultural and laboring class which really constitutes the backbone of our country. The pioneers, the reader can hardly have failed to notice, belonged to and married into the best Catholic families of the Cartwright's Creek and Rolling Fork settlements.

Today representatives of the early Kentucky families whom we have traced are scattered throughout the north, south, and west. Some are in the east. Whether in the home state or elsewhere, there have been but few defections from the faith among them; and these have invariably resulted from mixed marriages. All in all, the story is one in which those belonging to any of the lines laid before the reader should find no little consolation. Nay, it is a record of which they may be justly proud. The writer's hope and prayer are that it will serve as a guide for the generations yet to come.

www.ingramcontent.com/pod-product-compliance
Lightning Source LLC
Chambersburg PA
CBHW060536080526
44586CB00012B/750